BOYCOTTING PEACE

BOYCOTTING PEACE

Why Divestment is Turning Truth on its Head

Fred Taub

Balfour Books

First printing: February 2011

Balfour Books
Customer Service: +1 877 887 0222
P.O. Box 2180
Noble, OK 73068

ISBN: 978-1-933267-20-3

Cover and Interior by Brent Spurlock, Green Forest, AR

Printed in the United States of America

Please visit our website for other great titles:
www.balfourstore.com

To:

My parents,
Sam and Magda Taub

Acknowledgements:

So many people contributed to this book in countless ways, and it is simply impossible to name them all, so please forgive me if I leave anyone out. I would like to thank the following people: Alan Black, who taught me how to communicate in business; Steven Vendeland from Ambassador's Ink[1], the editing ninja; my editor-in-chief Jackie Gallo; Elisheva Creve, who always supplied refining comments; my radio partner Tzvi Turner, who puts up with me; Dennis Seaman, who has been called one of the 36; Virginia Gilley, a modest realist; Jay Weiss, who views the world with moral clarity; the quiet and thoughtfully opinionated Sally Weiss; my good friend Debbie Schlussel, who is wise beyond her years; Jerry Gordon, who personifies wisdom; Chris Morton, who takes no prisoners; Joe Coste, Tom Coste, and their staff at Amy Joy Donuts, where I spent many nights writing and editing; Gary Grunwald, who still calls me "HaRav";

1.www.ambink.com

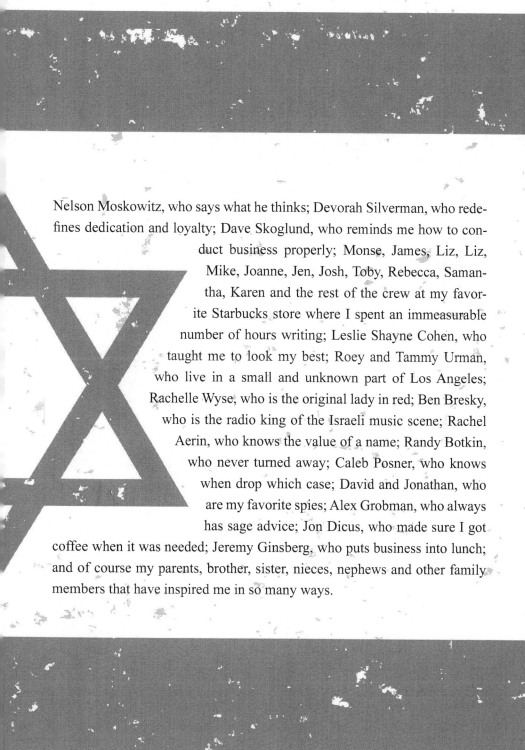

Nelson Moskowitz, who says what he thinks; Devorah Silverman, who redefines dedication and loyalty; Dave Skoglund, who reminds me how to conduct business properly; Monse, James, Liz, Liz, Mike, Joanne, Jen, Josh, Toby, Rebecca, Samantha, Karen and the rest of the crew at my favorite Starbucks store where I spent an immeasurable number of hours writing; Leslie Shayne Cohen, who taught me to look my best; Roey and Tammy Urman, who live in a small and unknown part of Los Angeles; Rachelle Wyse, who is the original lady in red; Ben Bresky, who is the radio king of the Israeli music scene; Rachel Aerin, who knows the value of a name; Randy Botkin, who never turned away; Caleb Posner, who knows when drop which case; David and Jonathan, who are my favorite spies; Alex Grobman, who always has sage advice; Jon Dicus, who made sure I got coffee when it was needed; Jeremy Ginsberg, who puts business into lunch; and of course my parents, brother, sister, nieces, nephews and other family members that have inspired me in so many ways.

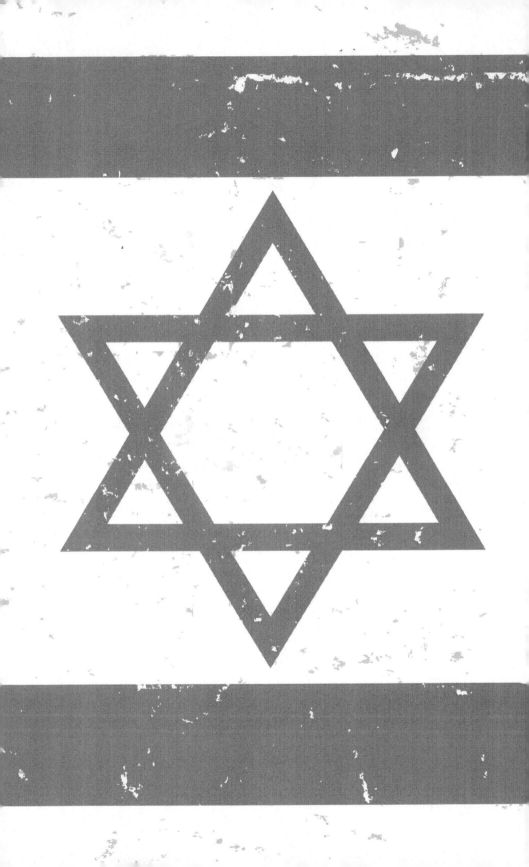

Preface

My interest in boycotts developed from my early fascination with people's reactions to advertisements. Some people with similar interests become psychologists, advertising executives or sales professionals; however, I have always gravitated towards running small businesses, sometimes as a side job, while working full-time. I have long been an activist too, someone who believes that it is more important and rewarding to be involved in one's community rather than simply being wealthy and donating money to various causes without any kind of emotional investment.

At times I would play the stock market game and observe people's reactions to the news and how they affected the price of particular securities; however, I would not purchase stocks because I believed in investing in my own business ventures. I grew particularly fond of watching businesses in financial trouble. This interest did not stem from any morbid curiosity; rather, I wanted to see how businesses recovered from having bad names or reputations. People like Lee Iacocca, who reshaped the nearly extinct Chrysler car company to reach new highs, and Victor Kiam, who went on television promoting Remington Razors with the line, "I liked it so much, that I bought the company," inspired and impressed me. I saw how people responded to these ads and pitchmen because they believed them. It was more than the power of advertising: it was consumer trust in people with whom they could relate.

Trust in television advertising started in the early days of broadcasting. In those days, radio and television show hosts would put their own names only on the products they liked, attaching their own reputation to such products. These shows would only have a single product sponsor, and the product's success often depended on how much the consumers trusted the program's host, who put his reputation on the line when pitching these goods. Today, many of these products still exist thanks to the consumer's earlier trust in the advertising and the honesty of the programs' hosts. As single product shows gave way to multiple advertisers on television and radio, so too did individual trust. Unless it is a fundraiser for a charitable cause, products soon began to be pitched by unknown actors, not people who put their own credibility behind products, a trend which started long before product liability fears.

In the 1970s, television ads became ridiculous as people would act completely out of character and not remotely like normal individuals involved in real life situations. Though customers still purchased advertised items, consumers seldom felt a personal attachment to ads or products. One exception to this rule is children, who loved their favorite characters that promoted breakfast cereals and toys, ignoring the nature of this advertising. The dichotomy of adults verses children's reactions to advertising proved the value of personal attachment advertising pitchmen more than the products they endorsed. For example, Betamax video tape was far superior to VHS tape, yet VHS tape won that media battle due to better marketing.

Beginning with Dave Thomas of Wendy's fame, these days we are seeing a resurgence in personally pitched ads, and this rebirth has been growing ever since. Even radio has changed dramatically. Gone are the days of Wolfman Jack and other "radio voices"; instead, we now hear naturally plain voices speak to us about various topics while they endorse the advertisers' products. People like real, live, honest people and today we see radio talk show hosts promoting products, while openly proclaiming they put their names on the items.

People are seeking this kind of trust, and when they receive an email about a boycott for some reason, they often believe the message provided because it is written passionately and seemingly with accurate information. However, the question remains: what is the truth? Emails written by anonymous or unknown people are like unsigned checks—they are worthless. My examination of consumer trends and later boycotts has inadvertently made me an expert in boycotts, consumer reactions to boycotts, boycott preventions, and responses.

While investigating boycotts, I came across the Arab boycott of Israel, which has been long forgotten after the passing of a 1977 law restricting foreign boycotts. People apparently forgot about the Arab boycott of Israel or really didn't care. However, I discovered the world's largest boycott was greatly affecting everyone's daily lives, regardless of their religion or where they lived, because it was the fundamental and underlying basis for sustaining the Arab-Israel conflict. No other single boycott had such an affect on any product, let alone world markets.

The purpose of this book is to demonstrate how the Arab boycott of Israel is still being used to spread and foster both the greater Arab-Israel conflict and anti-Semitism in general. I fully explain how businesses and people have been used as pawns to spread hate unknowingly and unwittingly. My goal is simply to show people the truth. Good people should not allow themselves to be used as instruments of hate, and I refuse to sit back and allow those who hate to flourish in their destructive desires. In this text, I expose this boycott as an anti-Semitic method to destroy Israel, and I provide official Arab boycott documentation to demonstrate this point.

Peace can never be achieved through any kind of boycott. If you want peace with someone, you must sit down with then for a cup of coffee—either metaphorically or literally—and not draw lines in the sand preventing coexistence.

Fred Taub
October, 2010

Contents

The Arab Boycott of Israel and Middle East Peace

CHAPTER 1

Let's face it: You cannot have peace with someone that you would not sit down with for a cup of coffee. It's that simple. Just having coffee together does not ensure peace, and neither is peace sustainable simply because you have two signatures on a piece of paper. Politicians like to view peace on paper agreements for one reason—it makes them look like heroes—but the reality is that this kind of peace on its own, is an illusion. Think of it this way. If you were to build a house from scratch, you would not install plumbing fixtures before the concrete foundation had been poured. Not only would it make no sense, but also it would be impossible. The finishing touches of a new house happen after all structural walls are erected and the roof is complete. Just like steps need to be taken in a prescribed order to build a house, there is a natural order to building peace between nations. You must clear the obstructions before you can begin building the foundation for a sustainable peace. These pages will identify the single biggest obstruction to peace in the Middle East, and there will never be any harmony in that region until this obstruction is eradicated.

Since elected politicians have relatively short terms in office, they know they must point to various successes to get themselves and their political party reelected. No matter what the election, the conflict in the Middle East is always a dominant issue, and politicians expect and accept failure, provided that they can push blame onto a third party, in particular the opposition party. There is no greater political victory than being the person seen as bringing peace to the Middle East. Brokering peace has its rewards, such as receiving the Nobel Peace Prize along with international acclaim and recognition, not to mention a big money book deal. All politicians know that quick fixes to complex problems are ineffective, but they also know that they will not receive the Nobel Peace Prize unless they create the illusion of progress toward solving the Middle Eastern conflict. These politicians are also aware that subsequent administrations will not follow their leads for long because each politician wants their own name on whatever they work on, simply so they get the credit. The nature of politics demands quick solutions, which is why politicians focus on relatively new issues such as who lives on which hilltop, rather than addressing the underlying factor and root instigation of the Middle East conflict: the Arab boycott of Israel.

In recent years, the Arab boycott of Israel has been intensified by advocates of divesting, withdrawing, and ceasing investments from Israel. Divestment is just another word for a boycott, and people are recruited to join that campaign under the false pretense that it will bring to peace to the Middle East. These individuals and businesses do not generally understand that the divest-from-Israel campaign is a direct subsidiary of the Arab boycott of Israel, and none of its various manifestations are new either. Since it is an integral part of the Arab-Israeli conflict, one must understand the origin of the Arab boycott of Israel, a term the Arab nations coined. From there, we can understand the problems in that region and then begin initiating true peace proceedings. In examining the origins of the Arab boycott, it sometimes helps to look at historical accounts as they relate to the history of the Middle East, in order to rectify false claims that support this unnecessary and anti-peace and destructive boycott.

Who Lives There?

In his 1867 book *The Innocents Abroad*, Mark Twain described the region as,

> A desolate country whose soil is rich enough but is given over wholly to weeds. A silent, mournful expanse. We never saw a human being on the whole route. There was hardly a tree or a shrub anywhere. Even the olive and the cactus, those fast friends of a worthless soil, had almost deserted the country.

While Mr. Twain was known for his satire, his comment does make the point about how desolate the area appeared; however, there has always been a small contingent of Jews in Jerusalem and Tzvat. Thirty years after Mr. Twain published his book, the First Zionist Congress was held in Basle, Switzerland. This landmark meeting brought together the top Jewish leaders and writers from all over the world under one umbrella for the first time in nearly 2000 years. The movement to reestablish Israel would then begin to gain considerable momentum.

In 1901, the Jewish National Fund (JNF) was established as the primary body to raise money worldwide and to purchase land in the Palestine region of the Ottoman Empire for establishing of the state of Israel. Bulk land purchases were relatively easy at the time since the vast majority of the land was held by absentee landlords, all of whom saw no use for the desolate land Mr. Twain had earlier referred. After land was purchased, money donated to the JNF was used to turn the barren land into productive agricultural fields, thus coining the phrase "making the desert bloom." With few resources available, pioneering Jews realized the necessity of working together to build farms. This was the origin of the Kibbutz movement, which were small collectives of land where people shared everything and grew crops needed to feed the people, even those outside the Kibbutz farm collectives.

The Kibbutz concept was not a Jewish invention; rather, it was based on the Soviet Union state farms in which individuals or families who worked on the larger state farms were also allocated a small portion of land for their own personal farming. The problem with the Soviet Union farming system was that the small private plots produced the vast majority of agricultural goods, whereas the larger state farms produced a nominal amount. Farmers would be responsible for directly selling these goods in small farmers' markets, thus creating small windows of capitalism within the socialist/communist system. The Kibbutz movement grew tremendous amounts of produce in those pioneering days of Israel, due to the pioneering and ideological Zionist spirit of the Jews at the time. Today, the Kibbutz is primarily a memory; just like in the former Soviet Union, people now produce more and better products—they literally benefit from the fruits of their labor. Only a few Kibbutzs[1] remain today, not only because Israel's economy is no longer agriculturally based, but also and primarily because the Kibbutz is simply unprofitable in today's economy. Private farms thrive in Israel; in fact, there is a great global demand for Israeli cheese, wine, snacks and fresh produce.

The land purchased by the Jewish National Fund is well-documented. Because the JNF was an official arm of the soon to be established state of Israel, to this day the Israeli government owns the vast majority of the land. The Israel Land Trust is responsible for managing the property and for granting long-term leases for individual and business usage. From time to time, proposals to privatize the land appear on Israel's political landscape; however, I highly doubt any such proposal will be seriously acted upon when you consider the current political situation. While some relatively small parcels of land in Israel have remained out of the hands of the Israel Land Trust, individual Jews have purchased much of that land, and the state of Israel has recorded these transactions. In fact, some of the land titled to Jews in Israel has ended up behind political barricades. This is most common in Hebron; here, Jews may not even live on their own property if located in areas that politicians have

---

1.Kibbutzim in Hebrew

assigned to the Palestinian Authority, which forbids Jews from their adminis-trated lands. Paradoxically, many Arabs own private land and live peacefully in Israel. So if you hear claims about "Israeli apartheid," a simple look at the facts will tell the real story—this will be explored later in greater depth.

Just like the California gold rush and pioneer expansion in the Western United States, entrepreneurs and prosperity seekers followed Jews to the Pal-estine region of the Ottoman Empire—the land Mark Twain characterized as barren. Other than those of the Jewish faith, Europeans and Americans were generally not attracted to the area. The Jewish agricultural influx into the region became a magnet for non-Jews, primarily Arabs who wished to improve their station in life. While most of the world thought it was crazy to move to the harsh and barren Palestine region, nomadic Arabs felt comfortable; therefore, as the Jewish presence grew in the formerly barren region, so too did the Arab presence. Even though many Arabs were prospering in the area, they were offended by the reality that Jews were planning a state; ironically, some of the most vocal Arabs were those who had moved into the Palestine region for the economic opportunities that the Jews had created. Although many Arabs felt that allowing a Jewish presence there was an affront to Islamic law, they still accepted the prosperity the Jews brought and created.

Many Arabs claim their families lived in the Palestine region of the Turk-ish Ottoman Empire for centuries as part of an Arab presence, but if that were the case one may want to ask for the Arabic name of the land. The name of the region, even to Arabs, is Palestine, a word derived from a 12th Century French word name for the Philistines, and has nothing to do with Arab or Islamic cul-ture. The only old Arabic name for anything in the region is Al-Quds, the name of the mosque of the Dome of the Rock, but not the city of Jerusalem itself and certainly not the Palestine region. The Arabs adopted the Palestine name from the Ottoman Turks, who were not Arab, and then claimed the French name as Arabic. The word 'Palestine' is neither in the Koran nor is it linguistically Arabic in any way.

The Koran claims that once Muslims rule a land, it earns the distinction of being Dar Al-Islam, or Islamic territory, and non-Muslims may never rule it. Alternatively, land that Muslims never controlled is called Dar Al-Harb in Islam, or land of chaos, since they had never ruled it. Since the Ottoman

Empire was mostly, though not completely, considered Dar Al-Islam, Arabs refused to tolerate even the idea of establishing a Jewish state in any part of the former Ottoman Empire, even though the Palestine region was never under Islamic control. Islamic leaders, however, wanted their own empire without Jews, and regional Muftis, or Islamic scholars, declared the land designated to become Israel as Islamic without any historical support. Still, the only established Islamic presence in the region was the Mosque at the Dome of the Rock, a building that was essentially run-down and abandoned when Mark Twain made his journey. The opulent upgrades to the previously dilapidated building that we see today were only made for the purpose of staking an Islamic claim to that location. Remember, while the rock site is mentioned in the Koran, the city of Jerusalem is never mentioned; therefore, the city of Jerusalem is not holy according to Islam. Although the Ottoman Empire controlled the Palestine region at one point, no independent Palestine nation had ever been established. In fact, it would have been impossible for one to have been established because there were no occupants to run any such nation. Ottoman Empire coins from the 1920s can be found on internet auction websites with the word Palestine in Arabic, Hebrew and English, thus clearly establishing who controlled the region. The fact that Al-Quds is the name of the mosque of the Dome of the Rock and the city of Jerusalem itself has no name in Islam or Arabic, clearly indicates who had and still has a direct connection and claim to Jerusalem.

In her book *Jerusalem 1913: The Origins of the Arab-Israeli Conflict*, Pulitzer Prize winning, *Wall Street Journal* writer, and author Amy Dockser Marcus claims that the Arab-Israeli conflict started with a dispute over orchards. But strife had begun as early as 1910, because many Arabs did not want Jews there. Then in 1921, as the Jewish presence was growing in the Palestine region, a general boycott of Jewish interests in the region was declared. As Kennan Lee Teslik described in his book *Congress, the Executive Branch, and Special Interests—The American Response to the Arab boycott of Israel*, the boycott was designed to starve Jews out of the region before the state of Israel could be established. Faced with this, JNF donations increased as Jews throughout the world united to help their fellow brethren. While there had been various physical attacks by Arabs on Jews in the area for years, this boycott was the first organized warfare effort. I call this "economic warfare" because that is what it is, an economic war to starve Jews out. The central organizing body of the Arab boycott of Jewish interests in the region was the Arab Congress; which was renamed the Arab League once other Arab nations were formed. To this day, the Arab League remains the unifying and governing body of the Arab world and retains its founding principal of the eradication of Jews from the Middle East.

States Are Born

When speaking about the Middle East, Arabs like to give people the false impression that their nations were long-established. Most people do not realize that even Egypt is a relatively recently formed country, gaining its independence from the United Kingdom on February 28, 1922. Historically, the former Ottoman Empire, which presided over the land that Egypt encompasses, officially disbanded on October 29, 1923, due to the end of World War I. Saudi Arabia has a different origin, and today celebrates the unification of the kingdom, which occurred on September 23, 1932. On this day, King Saud married one bride from each tribe in his region, thus uniting several tribes into one kingdom. This polygamy has resulted in about 20,000 or more princes, princesses and their families living off the kingdom's oil revenue; the personal demands of the children are a key factor in Saudi oil prices. Egypt and Saudi Arabia are far from the center of what is now Turkey, which gained its independence on October 29, 1923, and is the direct successor state to the Ottoman Empire. The excessive distance to the heart of the Ottoman Empire, especially for that era when you consider the poor communications at the time, facilitated the early independence of Egypt and Saudi Arabia. The European powers, who were temporary caretakers of the land, either chose or had the capacity to do only so much because they had to pay for their temporary administration of the land. This was an undesired outcome and responsibility of World War I.

The Palestine region of the Ottoman Empire consisted of what is now Jordan and Israel, a land originally meant to be entirely a Jewish homeland as set aside by the League of Nations, which preceded the United Nations. However, that land was later split in two to both fulfill a British promise to the Hashemite sheik for his own land and to separate Jews from Arabs to prevent further land conflicts. The term "sheik" is still to this day largely misunderstood outside the Arab world. While the British thought of that title as a king, a sheik can be anything from a head of a single household to an actual king. Without a nation there, however, there was no kingdom to rule; thus, the British were fooled by the title. The British idea was to create both a "Jewish-Palestinian state" and an "Arab-Palestinian state" in the Palestine region of the former Ottoman Empire. Despite receiving about 75% of the Palestine region, the Arab world would soon demand more; not because they had any legitimate claim to the land, but because the Arabs just didn't want Jews there. This *No Jews Allowed* attitude prevails even today.

The Hashemite Kingdom of Jordan was originally named Trans-Jordan by the British, essentially meaning the eastern or other side of the Jordan River. It was cut off from what was meant to be an entirely Jewish state. The explanation was that Jordan was named for the river because it was on the other side of the river and not for the land itself. In fact, the name "Jordan" is a translation of *Yarden* from the Jewish bible and there is no actual Arab name for it. The name "Jordan" as a country was an afterthought that stuck and still happens to speak volumes about how Israel was created. Jordan had its independence from the League of Nations mandate, which the United Nations under British administration adopted on May 25, 1946. On May 14, 1948, Israel, being the land west of the Jordan River, gained its independence from the League of Nations mandate that the United Nations had adopted. These dates and years are important because they demonstrate the fact that the Arab boycott of Israel was in place 27 years before the formation of Israel, and that Israel was not carved out of any "Palestine" nation. If anything, it proves that a Palestinian-Arab nation called Jordan was carved out of the land designated to become Israel, the exact opposite of what the Arabs publicly claim.

The logical question now is to ask where was the country of Palestine to which the Arabs lay claim? The answer is that history proves there was never a nation called Palestine. There was never a capitol of any nation called Palestine. There was never a currency for any nation called Palestine. There was never a government of any nation called Palestine. If you want proof that Jews were the actual Palestinians, all you have to do is look at old newspapers and books. There, you will see the term "Palestinian" historically referred exclusively to Jews living in the Palestine region of the then former Ottoman Empire. Most major Jewish organizations, including the Jewish National Fund, referred to themselves as being "in Palestine" since that was the name of the region, not any state, and Israel had not been officially declared yet. The Arabs living on the eastern side of the Jordan River were officially called Trans-Jordanian.

Proof of this can be seen in a series of books called the *Palestine Yearbook*, renamed the *Israel Yearbook* in 1948, which the Zionist Organization of America published. Each annual edition contained detailed lists of activity in the region as well as statistics and worldwide Jewish activity related to the soon-to-be-created State of Israel. The 1945 *Palestine Yearbook*, for example, clearly shows that many Jewish organizations in the area referred to themselves as Palestinian or living in Palestine because that was the name of the region. Examples of such organizations include the following: the Jewish Agency for Palestine, an Israeli governmental institution later renamed the Jewish Agency, the United Palestine Appeal, later renamed the United Jewish Appeal, then the United Jewish Communities and recently renamed the Jewish Federations of North America, which is the major fundraising arm of the Jewish community in North America; the American Palestine Jewish Legion; and the list goes on. The Arabs only adopted the name "Palestinian" after the Jews abandoned it to use the name "Israel".

In fact, the official identification and passports issued to Jews who migrated to the region before Israel's independence were all marked as being Palestinian; meanwhile, Arabs were identified as being from various regions such as Syrian or Trans-Jordanian. Arabs were documented as being from everywhere except Palestine and were not considered Palestinian. The naming of Jews as Palestinian goes back to the Balfour Declaration of 1917, the official British policy of establishing the Jewish homeland. Naturally that name came as recognition that the land was the Palestine region of the Ottoman Empire. Because Jews were meant to settle the then barren land, the appropriate political name for the Jews, therefore, was simply Palestinian. Additionally, designating that barren land for a Jewish homeland was easy since nobody else wanted it or claimed it for a state. The Arabs did not do so at the time of the Balfour Declaration, and they especially did not do so when accepting Trans-Jordan as a settlement to land demands. The creation of Jordan was the original land for peace deal. Clearly, the name Palestinian originally referred to Jews, not Arabs. In response, Arabs now argue that this was colonial imperialism; however, if any-thing, it was decolonization since the League of Nations had mandated that the British create a government and then leave the area. This is similar to what the U.S. desires to do in Iraq—create a stable government and leave. That is hardly colonialism or imperialism.

It was only in recent years that Jordan ceased its claim to the land referred to as the "West Bank" in the media. Yehudah V'Shomron is the actual name for the two regions in Hebrew, stemming from the Bible, which translates to Judea and Samaria. These areas have no regional names in the Koran, just Biblical Hebrew names such as the Binyamina region, which was named for the tribe the land was assigned. After 30 years of Israeli rule, Jordan revoked the citizenship of their compatriots in Judea and Samaria, effectively leaving them stateless. This political move was meant to bolster claims for the inde-pendence of the Palestinian Authority, despite the PA not having internation-ally recognized passports. The move was meant to facilitate the creation of a second Arab-Palestinian state carved out of "Palestine" for Arabs; however, the failure of the Palestinian Authority to create a state hurt the political clout of the stateless Jordanians. By officially abandoning all claims to the land and citizenship of their people, Jordan jettisoned all their citizens over whom they had no political control and effectively created a Palestinian Arab constituency of the Palestinian Authority. For Jordan, this had the added benefit of removing the same type of radicals from their kingdom that had created a very unstable Gaza, thereby protecting the Jordanian kingdom from the real threat of a radi-cal overthrow.

When the state of Israel was declared on May 14, 1948, the boycott of Jewish interests in the region was in chaos. The Arab boycott had failed to starve out the Jews or prevent Israel from being established, but that was far from the end of the boycott. Syria, a nation that separated from French admin-istration under the League of Nations mandate and whose Independence Day was on April 17, 1946, took the active lead but had other plans to destroy Israel militarily while leading the Arab boycott's revitalization and expansion. Despite being attacked by the Arab nations' militaries on its Independence Day on May 14, 1948, Israel had been under economic attack for 27 years prior and faced countless Arab raids reminiscent of European pogroms. Until the day of Israel's independence, Jews around the world had been under attack just for being Jewish. Jews had hoped the establishment of Israel, which was thought of as the world's only safe haven for Jews, would inherently curb anti-Semitism globally. That hope faded quickly.

Terror, Inc.

The Palestine Liberation Organization (PLO) was established in 1964, a full 16 years after Israel had become an independent nation. The gap in years further indicates that the motivation to create an independent Palestinian state is neither based on the preexistence of any state actually called Palestine nor on the hope of a peaceful coexistence. The PLO became a household name in 1972 when the world was glued to their television sets. The "Black September" organization, a subgroup of the PLO that Yasser Arafat directed, took Israeli athletes hostage at the Munich Olympics. Before the Olympics that year, Jews in Israel and around the world were debating if Israel should participate in the Olympics in Germany considering the Holocaust had only occurred 30 years before and was all to fresh in the memories of survivors, soldiers, and other civilians alike. Israel went to the Munich Olympics in the name of international brotherhood and with multiple assurances of security for its athletes. Despite this, the Israeli wrestling team, including American citizen David Burger from Cleveland, Ohio, was brutally murdered in the name of creating a "peaceful" Palestinian state.

Several years and terrorist attacks later, the PLO attempted to overthrow the Hashemite Kingdom of Jordan. The attempt failed and the PLO was exiled to Lebanon, which until then was a vacation destination. The PLO, under Yasser Arafat's leadership, turned Lebanon into a war zone. While Southern Lebanon became the launching ground for terrorist attacks on Israel and the centrally located city of Beirut had become very dangerous, the Bekkah Valley of Lebanon remained protected since that was where heroin is produced. The PLO turned Southern Lebanon into a terrorist staging area for raiding parties and rocket attacks. Several years after the PLO effectively controlled Lebanon, Israel could no longer accept the pressure of terrorism against Israeli citizens and went into Lebanon to clear out the terrorist plague once and for all. As Israel was approaching Beirut, President Reagan called Prime Minister

Menachem Begin and demanded Israel not send any troops into Beirut and that the U.S. be allowed to remove the PLO terrorists from the region. Israel complied with the U.S. request and, in the process, many American soldiers lost their lives saving the lives of PLO terrorists, who would later return to terrorize Israel. Many analysts believe that had Israel fought just one more day and gone into Beirut, the PLO would have been destroyed for good, saving countless Israeli lives. In the process of the war, Israel captured hundreds of Soviet tanks and thousands of Soviet rocket propelled grenades, clearly indicating a full assault on Israel has been in the works and not just minor terrorist attacks.

He Was Only 24

One of the most shocking cases of anti-Semitism prior to Israel's establishment was the case of Shlomo Ben Yosef, whom the British had hanged in the Palestine administered region for having the audacity to defend Jews from a planned attack by Arabs. Born Shalom Tabachnik on May 7, 1913, to a poor family in Lutzk, Poland, Mr. Ben Yosef attended the local Cheder, or Jewish religious school. Tired of all the "Zhid" or "dirty Jew" slurs he heard when growing up, he joined the Betar movement, which eventually grew into the Likud Party of Israel. Betar instilled Jewish pride, a pride which was missing in his shtetle life of Europe where pogroms were the norm. The Zionist visionary Ze'ev Vladimir Jabotinsky had created Betar to both be the first Jewish army in 2,000 years and prepare Jews to become pioneers for the soon-to-be-formed Jewish state. In 1937, Mr. Ben Yosef smuggled himself into the land entrusted to the British to form the new state of Israel because the British suddenly restricted Jewish immigration to the future Israel in order to slow the process of launching the state. My father, an Auschwitz survivor who was in the Palestine region prior to 1948, explained that the British saw the land as being a last bastion of their empire that they wanted to keep. My father further explained that, from his firsthand experience, he learned the British administration and soldiers were more interested in making money in the region than anything else. The British, he said, also had no love for the Jews and therefore had no incentive to facilitate the creation of Israel.

The anti-Semitic British attitude toward Jews was not isolated. The 1976 movie "Voyage of the Damned" is the story of the S.S. St. Louis, a ship that sailed in 1937 with Jews trying to escape Nazi Germany. Sadly, the ship was turned away, forcing the Jews onboard to return to Germany to face certain death at the hands of the Nazis. It is a must see, true-story movie that exemplifies how anti-Semitism was rampant worldwide. Jews were turned back despite governments fully knowing the fate they were condemning Jews to. The creation of a modern Jewish state was seen by many as the only way to have a safe haven for Jews, yet the years leading up to Israel's independence were fraught with some of the worst hatred of Jews ever.

Returning to the story of Mr. Ben-Yosef, he experienced some of the worst anti-Semitism one could face as a pioneer, at the hands of the British who were given the responsibility to create a Jewish state. On April 21, 1938, Mr. Ben-Yosef learned of plans for a pending Arab attack on Jews and decided to take a defensive stand. Mr. Ben-Yosef knew the British would not stop the attack, which put him in a dilemma. The official policy of the soon-to-be established Jewish nation was to work with the British; this led to the Jewish community policy of "Havlagah," or self-restraint. Just like in the European ghettos when faced with pogroms, Jews at the time were accustomed to accepting attacks and keeping quiet about them. Jews were told they would make things worse if they took any defensive stance in Europe, and that attitude prevailed in British Mandate Palestine; therefore, the British expected Jews to take any and all Arab attacks against them in silence. Mr. Ben-Yosef decided he could not sit idle as Jews were murdered in his homeland. Without intending to do so, Mr. Ben-Yosef crossed the line and proved to the world that Jews needed to defend themselves, because nobody else would.

To fend off the pending Arab attack, Mr. Ben-Yosef hid on a hilltop until he saw the approaching Arab attackers. He fired one shot in the air to scare them off. It worked. The attackers fled. Until that day, there had been no defensive moves by Jews against such Arab attacks. There was not even as much as a scratch on the would-be assailants who quickly fled the scene, yet Mr. Ben-Yosef was forced to go into hiding for several days because the British did not like the violation of the Jewish self-restraint policy and issued an arrest order for Mr. Ben-Yosef. He was discovered hiding in a cave and subsequently arrested, tried, and sentenced to death by hanging simply for being a Jew defending the lives of other Jews. At his trial, Mr. Ben-Yosef refused to acknowledge the authority of the British to rule the land, including the authority of the British to put him, as a Jew, on trial in the land of Israel. A standoff ensued. Although the British claimed they would let Mr. Ben-Yosef go free if he would recognize British sovereignty, few including Mr. Ben-Yosef believed that claim. There were several high-level appeals for his life because the sentence of death was issued for firing a warning shot into the air, not aimed at anyone, and without any injuries. Despite pleas from his mother in court, the British would hang Mr. Ben-Yosef on June 29, 1938, as he sang "Shir Betar," the "Song of Betar" in proud defiance of the British.

That day ushered in the end for British rule in the land they were entrusted to turn into the Jewish state. The hanging of Mr. Ben-Yosef sent the message to Jews in the region that the British neither could be trusted nor would they facilitate the creation of the Jewish state. While there were still political rivalries and methodology disagreements within the Jewish population, from that point on efforts shifted to get the British to leave rather than work with them. The pioneering Jews suddenly realized they had no foreign friends in their own land. While Mr. Ben-Yosef smuggled himself into the Palestine region alone, Jews across all political lines worked together to actively smuggle people into their own homeland because the British, in wanting to block the formation of Israel, severely limited Jewish immigration in the process. Arabs were boycotting Jews, who were being attacked not only in the land destined to be the Jewish state but also around the world.

Despite the League of Nations allocating the land to create Israel, Jews had to fight against all odds to have that promise fulfilled. The creation of Trans-Jordan was the first land concession by Israel, a failed British policy that created the first failed Arab-Israeli land for peace concept. Jordan's inception did not result in Middle East peace, as evidenced by its being one of the nations, along with help from British military officers, attacking Israel on its Independence Day. Moments after dancing in the streets commenced in celebration of the new Jewish state, the first in 2,000 years, sirens blasted. Celebration turned to fear as Israelis, who at the time had no real army to speak of, were under attack by all of their Arab neighbors. Israel's War of Independence actually began years before with a boycott to starve the Jews out of the region. Arabs did not want Jews there, yet their boycott failed to prevent Israel from being formed and war ensued. Had land for peace really been the goal of the Arab states, Israel would never have had its War of Independence in the first place. The land for peace concessions were not honored because the Arabs did not want Israel to exist or for the Jews to live there. They just wanted the land.

Shlomo Ben Yosef gave his life to teach the world, and in particular Jews, that despite promises, nothing had really changed. After 2,000 years of exile, which included severe religious persecution, Jews would not be safe in their own land even with a seemingly benign government. That harsh lesson was proven just a few months after the British hanged Mr. Ben-Yosef on June 29, 1938, with Kristallnacht, where dozens of German and Austrian Jews were murdered, and with tens of thousands sent to concentration camps on November 9 and 10, 1938. Just as the world saw with the land concessions that created Trans-Jordan in the name of peace, trusting or relying upon promises alone is deadly. While some Jews are willing to make that same land for peace gamble, knowing it has never worked in the past, the Arab response continues to be boycotts, terrorism and other anti-peace gestures.

Land for Peace

Israel's giving the Sinai Peninsula to Egypt in 1978 did not result in real peace either, but it did result in meaningless Nobel Peace Prizes. While there is some cross-border tourism between Israel and Egypt, the amount of tourism is statistically insignificant. The fact is there is no real friendship across the Israel-Egypt border. The demilitarized Sinai Desert was meant to be a buffer between the nations, yet Egypt violates that by allowing arms to be smuggled into Gaza for the purpose of attacking Israel, not to mention that modern infrastructure and technology makes crossing the Sinai Desert relatively easy. Speaking of which, Israel leaving Gaza did not create peace either. That was the third attempt at land for peace; it too has failed. Once again, these failures bring us back to the reason the Arabs keep trying to push their boycott: the Arabs have failed to destroy Israel with every attempt, even terrorism against women and children. The Arab boycott is also, at face value, an easy and inexpensive way to harm Israel, but in reality it only strengthened the resolve of

Jews to fight Arab anti-Semitism. Let's face it: war, terrorism and boycotts cannot be construed as acts of love.

The Arab boycott of Israel was originally a regional boycott, but the establishment of the Jewish state meant the boycott had failed, since Jews were not starved out as originally intended. That, coupled with a military loss by the Arabs on May 14, 1948, resulted in a rather upset Arab world. Israel still had few friends in the world, as anti-Semitism was rampant worldwide, including in the United States where the Ku Klux Klan had a strong following. Jewish pride started to emerge worldwide, even in Hollywood where Jews would change their names despite everyone knowing the actors' religion. Suddenly, some Americans began to distrust the loyalty of American Jews, due mostly to their dual loyalties to Israel and the United States. Many wondered which nation came first. A trick question also emerged: "Are you a Jewish American or an American Jew?" Jews could not easily answer this confusing question, which was its intention all along; in fact, it is still sometimes heard today.

The new wave of anti-Semitism resulted in an excuse for Americans to join the Arab boycott effort, thus inherently creating a global expansion of the original Arab boycott. Without land route trading partners, Israel could only trade with international partners by utilizing cargo ships, an added expense to imports and exports. Israel's trade difficulties were somewhat compensated by both the continued Jewish donations to support projects in Israel and also Jews worldwide seeking Israeli products out of pride. Of the original exports, some of the most popular goods were Jaffa oranges and Elite chocolate. From a consumer standpoint, other than tourism, there was no better way to get a taste of Israel than to sample the products of the country, which had an agricultural society in its early years.

The Arab boycott of Israel gained in strength after the establishment of the Central Boycott Office in Damascus. This office maintained and compiled the various national Arab boycott lists into a single comprehensive global blacklist of all companies conducting business either with or in Israel. Although originally a primary boycott, meaning Arabs would simply not purchase Israeli products, the work of the Central Boycott Office intrinsically expanded the Arab boycott to a secondary global boycott. Secondary boycotts are when individuals or groups boycott any business associated with Israel and even tertiary boycotts of those conducting secondary business with Israel. In an effort to stealthily blockade Israel from importing and exporting, the Arab boycott also included the list of ships that had ever docked in Israel, thus permanently banning those ships from ever docking at Arab ports. This shipping expansion inherently shifted the boycott burden and enforcement thereof to non-Arab shipping companies, which suddenly had to be very mindful of secondary boycotts if they wanted to do business in the Arab world. The Central Boycott Office got non-Arabs to do their work for them.

The Boycott Spurred Israeli Innovation

In terms of just land volume to determine where there are more trading opportunities, it is logical that businesses would prefer to trade with Arab nations, rather than Israel, since the Arab world is larger than Israel. Then there is the global oil market, a business sector the Arab nations control for the most part. These were major concerns by the 1960s, when the secondary boycott effort had created a global business war for which companies would have to decide of they would either trade with Israel or the Arab world, but rarely both. This forced Israel to buy its oil on the open market after it was offloaded to shore and then reloaded on ships that docked in Israel. Although it tried, the Arab world could not completely prevent Arab oil sold on the open market from being resold to and eventually used in Israel. Everything and everyone had a price, and getting around the boycott significantly added to fuel prices in Israel. The Arabs were not completely happy their oil ended up in Israel, yet they laughed to the bank while taking dollars from the nation. Besides, Arabs were more concerned about Israeli products ending up in their countries. Still, the world business community was put in the position of often being forced to take sides in a financial war aimed at destroying Israel economically. Oil sales proved that the Arab boycott was not going to be entirely adhered to because Israel has no choice but to pay more for oil, and it did.

Israel did not sit back and take the boycott without fighting back. In 1945, three years before the state of Israel was declared, the Jewish Agency and Israel's labor unions created what is now ZIM Integrated Shipping Services. The company was originally created to help bring Jews into what was designated to be Israel, and the company later became the primary shipping line to bring food into the country in defiance of the Arab boycott. The possibility of Arabs sinking cargo ships just for docking in Israel spurred the growth of ZIM, making it the shipping giant it is today. The advent of regular air travel put an end to ZIM's passenger service, and the company expanded to become a cargo-only company, as did other shipping lines. While ZIM may not have been planned as a key tool to fend off the boycott, its very existence allowed for the import and export of goods that would have otherwise never happened. In fact, it is possible that without this organization, Israel would have been even more isolated economically since its few international trading paths were landlocked by countries seeking its destruction. ZIM was built out of necessity due to Arab boycott pressure, and today it is key to Israel's economy.

The Arab Congress became the League of Arab States at their Cairo conference on March 22, 1945, which was about the time the six founding Arab nations were officially declared. Among the Arab League's stated missions, economic cooperation is most key, but only because the founding principal of the Arab League is to further the Arab boycott of Israel, to which the Palestinian Authority is signatory. Although the Arab League discusses issues other than the boycott, I have yet to see the minutes of any meeting that did not address or include a resolution supporting the boycott against the "Zionist entity," which Arabs call Israel, since they do not recognize its right to exist, let alone Israel's actual existence.

Since its inception in 1951, the Central Boycott Office (CBO) has maintained a list of blacklisted companies forbidden to sell products in the Arab world. It also maintains a list of ships that are forbidden to dock at Arab ports simply for having docked once in Israel. Amazingly, this includes situations where cargo possesses emergency supplies of lifesaving food or medicine for the Arab world. Though closely held, a copy of the official Saudi Arabia list did reach the United States Congress in the battle of creating U.S. Antiboycott laws. The list included American companies conducting business with or in Israel. Currently, the official list of companies boycotted includes businesses just because they are owned by Jews or have Jews in key management positions. Several groups supporting the boycott maintain their own independent lists of Jewish-owned companies they claim may have contributed to projects in Israel, encouraging guilt by association boycotts to punish the entire business irrespective of any Israel involvement or not. From a practical standpoint, the Arab boycott of Israel is not only expansive in scope, but also actively recruits Americans by lying about boycotts bringing peace. In the recruiting process, the truth of the Arab boycott of Israel is ignored, in that this boycott is economic warfare arm of Arabs against all Jews, not just Israel.

The CBO effectively made boycotting Israel a precondition for any company to conduct business in the Arab world, thus turning companies worldwide into pawns of Arab politics. More accurately, businesses that might consider working in the Middle East were held hostage to the political demands of Arabs to stay off the list. Naturally, businesses are not political entities and therefore have no reason to be involved in politics as entities, yet that is the mission of the Arab boycott: isolate every business from wanting to do business with Israel. It is never advisable for a business to put itself in a situation where it must decide who it wants for its customers while alienating other potential patrons, yet that is exactly what the CBO accomplished. This organization made working with Jews, and not just those in Israel, a bad idea; thus, the Arab boycott is undeniably anti-Semitic.

Rise of U.S.
Antiboycott Laws

CHAPTER 2

By the late 1960s, the Arab boycott of Israel began taking a firm hold in the United States, as did Persian Gulf oil. Middle East oil accounted for one-third of U.S. oil consumption at the time, and the fears that oil imports from the Middle East might be cut off because America remained friends with Israel became a common water-cooler topic. This was long before either the Alaskan oil pipeline built between 1974 and 1977 or the oil crisis during the Carter Administration, but it does illustrate the power and fear the Arab boycott instilled into American consumers. For the most part, Americans did not blame Israel for oil supply concerns, but there were lingering worries that America could be held hostage with the tightening of oil supplies for being friends with Israel. It took years for Americans to realize that the Arab world needed U.S. dollars to survive and transition into the modern world. Unbeknownst to Americans at the time, the Arab world felt hostage to America and Europe, the primary market for its only export—oil.

Israel's existence and military victories over the Arab nations changed the perception of Jews in the public eye, lending respect to American Jews for Israel's victories the way sports fans applaud a home town win. Americans felt an unspoken religious kinship with and admiration for the tiny Jewish state for its victories over the foreign oil barons. Personal hatred does not change instantly, but it did become less socially acceptable. This is not say anti-Semitism vanished; to the contrary, anti-Semitism still flourished and went underground as American Jews earned respect based on Israel's military victories, which showed the world that Jews would no longer be pushed around. Israel's victories in the 1967 Six Day War and the 1973 Yom Kippur War instilled a new sense of pride in Jewish students, a group which inherently always stuck together in schools for personal safety. Jews who had previously put up with anti-Semitic slurs in their schools suddenly found themselves in the social driver's seat; they would no longer accept anyone alienating their religious brethren. Americans too, stood tall in the face of the Arab world quest to control the world via oil as a result of these victories. Beginning in 1967, America put itself on the perpetual path to oil independence, which was only partly achieved with the Alaska oil pipeline.

Without intending to become involved in Middle-East politics, U.S. companies found themselves the victims of the Arab boycott by the most casual of business associations. The Arab boycott went as far as blocking all Arab business dealings with companies and individuals having offices in Israel, investing in Israel, just working with any Israeli, or being "Jewish" in any capacity. Considering that most people do not pay attention to these factors, many American companies fell victim to and/or engaged in the Arab witch-hunt of blacklisting Jews in businesses. The argument that the Arab world has a much larger consumer market than tiny Israel made adhering to the boycott very attractive from a business standpoint. However, the Arab and Israeli markets were both skyrocketing at the time, and businesses around the world wanted to take advantage of the biggest and best opportunities available. In many cases, they felt they had to make a choice of where they wanted to do business.

Although it was not addressed as such at the time, the shared Judeo-Christian values made it natural for both Christian and Jewish Americans to trust Israelis. For Jews, the fact that many American Jews had moved to Israel facilitated business communications in English. Also, many American Jews knew people or had relatives in Israel. For Christians, their loyalty initially stemmed primarily from Israel's protecting Christian holy sites and the rights of Christians to pray at those holy places; such protections are virtually nonexistent in the Islamic world. Together, Christians and Jews viewed the reestablishment of Israel as ushering in the Messianic age. By the time the 1960s emerged, Israelis were buying American goods and technologies at a feverish pace while American consumers were literally eating up high quality Israeli agricultural products, despite higher costs. On the business side, Israel published posters touting how they made the desert bloom, a campaign primarily designed to promote the export of Israeli irrigation systems. Ironically, these systems were developed out of need for self sufficiency and in defiance of the Arab boycott. Americans and Israelis mutually benefited from the trade that was growing on both sides, and in many cases businesses separated by an ocean became mutually reliant without consumers even realizing it.

As a result of conducting business with Israel, the Arab League blacklisted Sears, Coca Cola, Xerox and a number of other companies in 1966. The Coca-Cola Corporation was perhaps the biggest company to accidentally become involved in Middle East politics by opening a bottling plant in Israel; this opened the door for Pepsi to dominate the Arab soft-drink market. This battle not only framed the Arab boycott of Israel in the eyes of Americans, but also people world wide. When Pepsi became the only cola in the Arab world, Jews worldwide responded by boycotting Pepsi with people going out of their way to buy Coke products. This counter-boycott resulted in many American Jews refusing to even eat at restaurants serving Pepsi, and a "Boycott Pepsi" bumper sticker campaign emerged as a result.

The Coca-Cola Corporation responded in 1971 with what is viewed by many as one of the best all-time television advertising campaigns ever.

Originally called the "Hilltop Ad" when produced, the one-minute commercial featured young people from diverse backgrounds, ethnicities, and nationalities singing "I'd Like to Teach the World to Sing in Perfect Harmony." The song quickly became popular and was modified by removing the Coke brand name to become a non-advertisement pop music single first by the Hilltop Singers and shortly afterward a pop music sensation by the New Seekers. The song, which spoke of peace and featured the words "It's the real thing," made people feel good about brotherhood. Although the Coca-Cola Corporation will not say the ad was specifically aimed at the Arab boycott of Israel, there is no question the message covered it as part of Coke's brotherhood message.

To some, the Arab boycott of Israel was used as an excuse for openly acting upon their ingrained anti-Semitism; others saw engaging in the boycott as a justification to avoid being labeled as anti-Semitic. Anti-Semitism was socially frowned upon, but it still existed as demonstrated by the famous 1970s Nazi march in Skokie, Illinois. From a current perspective, not much has changed except that the Ku Klux Klan has its occasional public rally while Nazi groups hide in remote campsites. The Arab boycott was, however, used as a global weapon against all Jews and not just Israel. Merely being affiliated with Jews by working with a local Jewish company or even donating to the Jewish National Fund could result in the blacklisting of a business wanting to conduct business in the Arab world. These are the secondary boycotts, which are boycotts against parties doing business with Israel. While the primary boycott is a direct boycott against business dealings with Israel or Israeli companies, tertiary Arab boycotts also emerged against those working with people doing business with Israel. These tertiary boycotts are a xenophobic isolationist policy to avoid any contact with individuals or business entities with even the slightest connection to Jews and Israel.

The Arabs were essentially seeking a global economic battle between Jews and gentiles; this is reminiscent of the Nazi boycott of Jewish businesses that preceded Kristallnacht on November 9-10, 1938, when the Nazis burned Jewish stores and books. Today, the Arab boycott of Israel and the associated divest-from-Israel campaigns are doing the same, with a modern twist. Adherents are boycotting Jewish-owned businesses and labeling stores on the Internet, as opposed to spray painting windows; regardless if the business has any real connection to Israel. The Arab street calls this the "electronic Intifada" or war. Additionally, there is the academic boycott of Israel, which pushes the banning of Israeli professors, their books, and even lifesaving discoveries from being used anywhere in the world. The academic boycott is clearly the modern version of book burning since it is designed to ban ideas from Israeli or Jewish parties. As proof of the anti-Semitic nature of the academic boycott, Arab academics are specifically exempt from the boycott along with Christians and people of other faiths. The academic boycott of Israel specifically targets Jews the same way the Nazis specifically targeted Jews on Kristallnacht. As such, the academic boycott is clearly, completely and purely anti-Semitic in every way. The masked claim of not liking Israel, but liking other Jews is once again thrown out. In fact, the Arab boycott and its subsidiary divest-from-Israel campaign not only includes, but specifically targets American businesses, including New York-based Estee Lauder, Inc. This shows that the Arab boycott of Israel is aimed at Jews in general and not just Israel, unless the Arab world has an innate fear of makeup and hand cream.

U.S. dependency on Arab oil was growing with domestic demand when the 1973 Yom Kippur War broke out, when Israel defeated the Arab world with the help of military resupply by the United States. Still dumbfounded by their loss, which they also saw as an insult, the Arab world mainly blamed the United States. Losing yet again to Israel was more than the Arab world could accept, especially since they had declared a Jihad, or Holy War, and had put their faith in Allah as their sole factor in creating victory. Blaming the United States was the only recourse Arab leaders had available to save face in the eyes of their subjects, which also helped justify the existence of their dictatorships. The Arabs still had one more trick up their sleeves, and a new front in their economic warfare against Israel was about to emerge: holding oil hostage.

Previously in 1960, the Organization of the Petroleum Exporting Countries (OPEC) was formed. Arab nations dominated the group along with a few other countries, including Venezuela, to round off the 13 founding states. OPEC was officially intended to stabilize, which in actuality meant raise, the price of oil across the board. As a cartel, however, it was a monopoly backed by governmental authority, thus making it an international trans-governmental power difficult to defeat. OPEC was specifically designed to get non-Arab countries to help enforce the Arab oil-control policy. OPEC, which is primarily under the control of Arab nations, declared an oil boycott against the United States because it helped Israel during the October 1973 Yom Kippur War. The result in the U.S. was a stock market crash and recession, something the U.S. would not take silently. A grassroots push for action emerged. The OPEC concept was born from the Arab boycott of Israel, as both organizations were designed to control markets and free association in commerce. Not every OPEC country is signatory to the Arab boycott of Israel, mostly because not all OPEC countries are Arab. However, the basic concept of holding consumers hostage is the basis of both OPEC and the Central Boycott Office, the official arm of the Arab League that coordinates the Israel boycott efforts of all member states.

Meanwhile, the Central Boycott Office proved to the world that their boycott was purely anti-Semitic when it published its boycott principals, which contained direct references to all Jews as opposed to just Israelis. As time went on, public anti-Semitism in the United States grew and became more commonplace, while the Arab boycott of Israel was strengthening in the United States. In 1975, the U.S. Army Corps of Engineers was found to be complying with the Arab boycott of Israel by discriminating in contracts and complying with Saudi Arabian demands that all Jews be refused entry into the Kingdom. To this day, the Kingdom of Saudi Arabia, and most Arab countries for that matter, denies entry to Jews or anyone having an Israel stamp on their passport. American businessmen who need to travel to Arab countries after being in Israel will routinely request and receive temporary passports, or else they will be denied entry.

Nobody is suggesting that it has ever been safe for Jews to travel in Arab nations, but the official U.S. Army Corps of Engineers' participation and acquiescence in the Arab boycott of Israel evoked public outrage. This was the single largest case of official Federal Government discrimination after the passing of the U.S. Civil Rights Act of 1964. While there had been some interest in formulating Antiboycott legislation in 1965, public outrage over the U.S. Army Corps of Engineers case in 1975 hit a boiling point, especially considering rising oil prices and the renewed American demand to end the Arab boycott. Efforts to create Antiboycott laws reemerged but remained a distant hope due to the difficulties of passing legislation through Congress and getting it signed into law. Jewish lobby groups, therefore, made fighting the Arab boycott of Israel their number one priority.

In the hearings before the Subcommittee on Monopolies and Commercial Law of the Committee on the Judiciary House of Representatives, Ninety-fourth Congress, first and second sessions on H.R. 5246, H.R. 12383 and H.R. 11488 Arab Boycott, July 9, 1975 and April 8, 1976, a copy of an official document of the Chamber of Commerce and Industries, Jeddah, Kingdom of Saudi Arabia was submitted to Congress. These 69 pages documented the official Saudi Arabian Kingdom boycott list and the Directory of Boycotted U.S. Companies and Establishments, a tightly held list that was somehow released and became part of the Congressional record. This list was one of many that covered the entire world and contained companies you would expect like Coca Cola, along with small and relatively obscure businesses. These companies supplied larger businesses and established Jewish organizations that Arabs would not do business with, even though these firms had no direct Israeli connections. While the list contains some businesses that no longer exist, the contents are interesting. The list includes many entities that would probably not be engaged in foreign trade; however, if a company has economic dealings with these businesses for any reason, such as selling them several light bulbs, then that company may not have any business dealings in the Arab world whatsoever. In many cases, the entities are listed only because Jews are involved despite the company itself has no other connection to Israel, thus further proving the boycott is anti-Semitic in nature, not just against Israel.

The list includes:

- **Yeshiva University:** Based in New York City, Yeshiva University is a nonprofit Jewish religious school with a rabbinical program, and is Zionistic in nature. While the school and students may buy books and other religious items made in Israel, these are relatively small individual student purchases. Because it is included in the blacklist, all companies that hire the school's graduates, including hospitals and law firms, are ineligible from conducting trade with the Arab world. What makes this more absurd is that not all the students are

Jewish, as the school does not discriminate in that manner. This is a prime example of secondary and tertiary boycotts, since potential employees would have had a connection with an officially boycotted entity. Having a major school such as Yeshiva University on the official boycott list clearly indicates Arab nations are prescribing discrimination against Jews as a prerequisite to having any business dealings with or in the Arab world. Similarly, the United Synagogue of America's Committee on Jewish Education is also on the Arab boycott list, thus demonstrating that the education-based boycott is not limited to Orthodox Judaism.

- **Jewish War Veterans:** The JWV consists of U.S. Jewish citizens who were members of the Unites States Armed Forces and fought in foreign wars. The JWV is not engaged in foreign trade, is not Israeli-based, and is not is a subsidiary organization of the Israel Defense Forces. The only reason this organization could be on the Arab boycott list is because its members are Jewish. This is another clear indicator the Arab boycott of Israel is anti-Semitic in nature, as it bans anyone with any connection to the JWV simply because Jews are involved. Additionally, this is a slap on the face of all the brave men and women who have served in the American Armed Forces.

- **Brush-on Eye Shadow Company:** This business apparently no longer exists under this name. Banning cosmetic companies in general sends a message that anyone associated with women who use cosmetics from Jewish businesses results in their entire company being banned from trade with the Arab world. That may sound absurd, but the boycott element was demonstrated in August 2009 when the Oxfam charity fired "Sex and the City" star Kristin Davis from being their spokeswoman when she became the spokeswoman for Israeli-made Ahava Cosmetics. It was both a clear violation of the U.S. Antiboycott laws and also a case of discrimination, based on her free association with an Israeli company. Of course, that is unless you insist on believing the Arab world has an innate fear of hand cream.

- **American Committee for Bar-Ilan University in Israel:** By including this nonprofit education and scholarship fundraising organization in the list, the Saudi Arabian Kingdom is stating that those associated with people wanting to help others be educated in Israel are permanently banned from dealing with the Arab world. In fact, the Saudi list includes listing two offices of this nonprofit, educational organization so nobody would possibly be confused to think it would be permissible to deal with any one office and not the other. The inclusion of the American Committee for Bar-Ilan University in Israel, in the 1976 boycott list, clearly indicates the academic boycott of Israel was initiated prior to 1976; therefore, it has been an integral part of the overall boycott for at least 30 years. Academic boycotts of Israel are not a recent advent. This element of the boycott not only bans all associations with anyone donating to the school, but also all associations with the schools graduates and academic work produced at the university.

The inclusion of the anti-Semitic book burning measures into the Arab academic boycott of Israel is no accident. After WWII, some Nazi officers escaped war crimes tribunal charges by moving to Syria. This includes Alois Brunner, who had worked for Adolf Eichmann and was later put on trial in absentia in Paris in 2001. Many of these actual Nazis worked with the Syrian government, thus establishing a direct connection between the book burnings of Kristallnacht and the academic element of the Arab boycott.

- **B'nai B'rith Hillel Foundation:** Hillel, as it is commonly known since separating from its parent B'nai B'rith, primarily assists Jewish students on North American college campuses in various ways. Hillel helps students obtain kosher food while at school, hosts campus Jewish prayer services, facilitates campus activities and hosts local religious study classes. Hillel is included on the list due to the Saudi Kingdom's rejection and objection to Jews practicing Judaism. Hillel does not export anything other than perhaps hot meals to students in their own dining rooms, which are usually fewer than 100 feet from their own kitchen. The blacklisting of Hillel is not only another example of anti-Semitism in the Arab boycott of Israel, but also indicates the Saudi rejection of Judaism as a legitimate practice. This desire to block Jewish students from taking part in the most basic Jewish religious practices is inherently and explicitly anti-Semitic. In fact, the very same Saudi Arabian list also blacklists the entire B'nai B'rith organization, which is classified as a fraternal organization, as its primarily secular membership is engaged in social activities including human rights campaigns and services for senior citizens.

- **Four Roses Distilling Company:** I find it odd that an Islamic kingdom felt compelled to list a distillery that makes bourbon, since Islam expressly forbids alcoholic beverages. But the reason is simple—the company, founded by Paul Jones, Jr., who I doubt is Jewish, was bought by the Jewish-owned Seagram. In fact, this is not the only distilling company on the blacklist: Frankfort Distillers, the Monarch Wine Company and, of course, Seagram itself. The fact that the Israel boycott blacklist contains American hard liquor distilleries demonstrates the there is a witch hunt to find Jews in business. After all, the Arab world is not supposed to purchase, import into Arab countries, or consume alcoholic beverages. This inclusion demonstrates the high level of hypocrisy within the Arab boycott of Israel. Saudi Arabia only lists wineries, breweries, and distilleries as part of their boycott when those companies are Jewish-owned. This further proves the Arab boycott is not so much about keeping Israeli products out of the Islamic world as it is about damaging Jewish businesses worldwide by personal and religious association.

- **J. Levine Religious Supplies:** Known today as Levine Judaica, this is just one of the officially boycotted Jewish religious stores, yet again there is no reason for such businesses to be on the official Arab blacklist since Muslims do not generally buy Jewish religious items. The only reason to include stores that primarily sell prayer books and related items to Jews is to intimidate non-Jews. This overt anti-Semitism is yet another example of the Arab desire to isolate Jews economically. It is also a prime example of the Kristallnacht attitude of the Arab boycott of Israel: to single out Jewish businesses with a Jewish clientele and keep everyone else away from associating with that business. It is intimidation by design. It is the virtual spray-painting of the windows of Jewish businesses to identify and single out Jewish stores, just as the Nazis did to facilitate their Kristallnacht rampage against Jews. The same virtual Kristallnacht exists on the websites of the Israel boycotters, who go out of their way to identify and tag businesses as Jewish or having an Israel connection to justify primary, secondary and tertiary boycotts.

There are many other companies on the Arab boycott list that have nothing to do with Israel, beyond perhaps having Jews in leadership positions, thus further proving that the Arab boycott of Israel is anti-Semitic first, and anti-Israel second. Other companies include: Allstate Insurance of Illinois; the American Bird Food Manufacturing Corporation based in Chicago, the Connecticut General Life Insurance Company; Empire Pencil Company; Moon Drops Moisture Lipstick Company; and the list goes on. In fact, a casual look at the Saudi Arabian list clearly reveals that it consists mostly of American companies, along with a few U.S. branches of Israeli businesses. Let's face it: companies like Allstate Insurance of Illinois sell insurance in Illinois, not

Mecca, and they have no intrinsic connection to businesses in the Middle East whatsoever. The only way one can find a connection is to be paranoid enough to look past every cubical wall and see a Jew working there. Here, the Arab boycott lists and websites do that research for you.

The boycott of companies on the list is a prime example of a secondary boycott since these are not Israeli companies, yet the Arab world wants to punish these organizations for having business dealings with Israel. Boycotting anyone with business dealings with these companies is an example of a tertiary boycott; encouraging such boycotts is why the Central Boycott Office and other Arab nations' boycott offices track these firms and publish their lists. The Arab boycott was clearly designed to punish Jews and anyone associated with Jews, even if their association has nothing to do with Israel. From its inception, the boycott was meant to punish people for their active or desired association with Israel and Jews. It is fundamentally discriminatory based on religion and association, not just national origin. Since the end of the Holocaust, the Arab boycott of Israel has been the single leading anti-Semitic entity, putting it in the running for the world's single longest anti-Semitic event of all time.

After two years of wrangling in Congress and opposition by President Ford, the Import-Export Act Amendment of 1977 was passed and signed into law by President Carter on June 22, 1977. In not wanting to make a law specific for one situation—the Arab boycott of Israel—the new law essentially states that no U.S. persons may engage in foreign government sanctioned boycotts against nations friendly to the United States. The term "U.S. persons" means anyone either residing in the United States or conducting business in the United States and its territories. Therefore, non-U.S. citizens must abide by the law if they are technically U.S. persons; the law prevents any such person from engaging in a "foreign sanctioned boycott," meaning government-sanctioned. Not only do single Arab governments sanction this boycott, but indeed, all Arab nations endorse the boycott to some degree. The boycott is even coordinated between Arab states at the highest governmental levels. In signing the law, Congress and the President both asserted their foreign policy authority and stated that both the legislative and executive branches of the U.S Government establish foreign policy. They did not want individuals or groups creating *de facto* U.S. foreign policy by boycotts, a.k.a. economic warfare.

The law created the Office of Antiboycott Compliance in the Department of Commerce. Since the law deals with foreign trade, it naturally fell under import/export controls; however, the law can apply to domestic persons who are not engaging in foreign trade, a topic that will be addressed when discussing the divest-from-Israel campaign. According to the Office of Antiboycott Compliance, the law includes and covers agreements to refuse or actual refusal to conduct business with or in Israel, or with blacklisted companies; agreements to discriminate or actual discrimination against other persons based on race, religion, sex, national origin or nationality; agreements to furnish or the actual furnishing of information about business relationships with or in Israel or with blacklisted companies; agreements to furnish or actual furnishing of information about the race, religion, sex, or national origin of another person; and implementing letters of credit containing prohibited boycott terms or conditions; the supplying of information to further the Arab boycott of Israel; requiring vessel eligibility certificates; requiring certification that goods are not made in Israel; demands for certificates of boycott compliance and more. Therefore, knowing which companies are actually blacklisted can assist in prosecution, which is why having a copy of the blacklist is so vital.

The one thing the law did accomplish was to calm Jews by giving the impression the regulation would end all implementations of the Arab boycott of Israel, especially in the United States. The blocking of the Arab boycott, however, hardly occurred. For starters, the Arab League member states regularly vote to strengthen their boycott at their meetings, and participating states have found ways to work around the Antiboycott laws. The highlight of the violations is discussed in Chapter 6: "Origins of and the present day Divest-From-Israel / boycott campaign". Here, an Indiana law professor, who worked for Yasser Arafat, devised a campaign to spread the illegal boycott throughout the United States.

Arab Boycott of Israel Today

lmost immediately after the implementation of the Antiboycott laws, the Arab world found a way to get around the new American laws. Prior to the Antiboycott law, Arab nations had required declarations with each shipment stating that all products exported to them were not made in Israel. With the new law, all exports from the United States to every nation signatory to the Arab boycott of Israel now require certifications that the products are made in the United States. These days, most businesses do not realize why they must make the declarations; the demands for

"Made in the U.S.A." declarations mask the true intent of the Arab world. I have seen certificates of United States origin for products such as wood to be shipped to the Arab world. Wood is scarce in Israel, thus Israel would hardly be in position to export wood to the United States for reshipment to the Arab world anyhow. This however illustrates how all U.S. exports to the Arab world are closely monitored to insure compliance with the Arab boycott. Not surprisingly, the lumber company in question is not Jewish owned, nor does the owner probably realize he is surreptitiously complying with a foreign boycott through a workaround.

The certification requirement is in place as a blanket rule and prevents workarounds such as buying American goods with any Israeli components, regardless of the goods' countries of origin. Using the legal terminology, instead of requiring "negative declarations," or certificates, that none of the products of components of items exported to the Arab world are made in Israel, Arab nations started demanding "positive declaration" certifications that the entire product is made in the United States.

This positive declaration workaround by the Arab world effectively prohibits Israeli goods from entering the Arab world by the United States. Initially, the law halted the secondary and tertiary boycotts against Israel by boycotting people associated with or doing business with Israel, and, as we will soon see, the specific boycotting of Jews in general. For starters, the Antiboycott law forbids the supplying and requesting of information about supplier compliance with the Arab boycott of Israel.

Any American company that receives a request for information about its possible business dealings with Israel must report such requests for information to the United States Department of Commerce, Bureau of Industry and Security. This includes requests for information about any possible dealings that company may have with other companies, which may do business with Israel. This provision of the law turned out to be vital since it prevents intimidation to comply with the Arab boycott of Israel.

The Bureau of Industry and Security within the United States Department of Commerce prosecutes violators of the law. Compliance with the Arab boycott of Israel and even failure to report requests for compliance may result in heavy fines, the denial of export licenses and even imprisonment. Reports of such violations regularly appear on the BIS website, and I have consulted on cases where businesses have had requests for such information, including demands to drop contracts with Israeli companies to obtain Arab business.

In one case, a company contacted me about their contract negotiations with Saudi Arabia where the company was told they would have to drop an active construction project in Israel in order to get a far more lucrative bridge construction project contract in Saudi Arabia. In that case, the Saudi Arabian government promised the company to more than make up for any losses for not completing the project in Israel.

As a non-attorney who read the law, I informed the company of their legal requirement to report the request to the Department of Commerce and potentially the IRS. The Saudi Arabian government naturally didn't tell the construction company about the U.S. compliance or reporting requirement. By enticing the American company with promises they would make far more money than any losses they would face as a result of halting the Israeli project, Saudi Arabia did not appear to care about any potential legal problems or reputation damage to the American company. Therefore, I believe the American construction company may have specifically been under consideration for the Saudi Arabia contract to disrupt the project in Israel. This case clearly depicts the true nature of the Arab boycott—deceit, legal entrapment and economic warfare against Israel.

The masking of Arab boycott of Israel compliance requests is not seen as a problem by Arab companies as long as they do not have a presence in the Unites States. The law only applies to anyone with a presence in the United State; it cannot be enforced outside the Unites States borders. Additionally, foreign nationals with no presence in the United States who make such requests do not care about Americans, and there are no consequences for compliance or non-reporting. That is, unless Arabs use American companies as their patsy, disrupting the Israeli economy while destroying anyone else in the process.

Just having the law in place, however, calmed Americans to the point where the Arab boycott of Israel was all but forgotten about until March 2002. Around this time, I had launched Boycott Watch and subsequently Divestment Watch to monitor and report about boycotts, in particular consumer boycotts and the Arab boycott, two areas I had been monitoring for years. Divestment

Watch was designed to specifically concentrate on the Arab boycott of Israel and its subsidiary divest-from-Israel campaign. After working extensively on the topic, I got the Zionist Organization of America (ZOA) to assist with the campaign, composing a complaint letter to the U.S. Department of Commerce and a second letter to the same department signed by several Members of Congress. The Arab boycott of Israel and the subsidiary divest-from-Israel campaign were not seen as a priority by some Jewish organizations for years; however, recently it has become a hot topic. I can now accurately say "I told you so," as the Arab boycott of Israel is again creating *de facto* U.S. foreign policy, the very thing the Antiboycott laws were created to prevent.

The law does have some bite, but I get the impression the Office of Anti-boycott Compliance is highly understaffed, considering the number of pros-ecutions made compared to the number of cases. While there are some pros-ecutions, the $10,000-$100,000 fines usually do not match the level of profit that companies have made while complying with the Arab boycott. First-time offenders usually get their export license revoked; few ever end up in jail. The law and prosecution keep many people from taking part in the Arab boycott, but the boycott still thrives. I have sent complaints to the Office of Antiboy-cott Compliance regarding the domestic divest-from-Israel campaign, which is clearly covered under the law, but the small overworked staff has not yet had the time to deal with that.

On April 15, 2003, the New York Post published an article by Paul Tharp titled "Apple Gets Bruised in Arab-Israel Fight". In it, Mr. Tharp notes that an Apple Computer in the Middle East was discovered to contain a battery made in Israel, outraging the technician who accidentally discovered it. Even hav-ing a single Israeli component in a computer is intolerable to those upholding the Arab boycott of Israel. The local distributor, who was not a subsidiary of Apple computer, agreed to replace all Israeli components free of charge as the company did not want to be seen as distributing or condoning Israeli compo-nents. I called Apple Computer to enquire about the report, and the company refused to comment about the origin of components used in their computers, which is odd for several reasons. First, anyone can open a computer and see who made a battery so that is not a trade secret. Second, Apple had not been in obvious compliance with the Arab boycott, but acquiescence to the new demand is possible. Third, not speaking to media draws more attention than answering basic questions. My inquiry about Arab boycott compliance was not to further the Arab boycott so they did not need to report that to the Department of Commerce, but their silence raises questions about possible future plans to boycott Israeli components in general. This is especially important since Apple computers are popular in Arab countries because Intel and Microsoft both develop products in Israel, thus are automatically boycotted. The battery issue may foreshadow Arab boycott compliance by Apple, even if only in computers destine for export. Apple is on my watch list, and is hopefully on the BIS watch list as well. This is a prime example of where the demand of a certification stating all components are made in the U.S.A. would be used to circumvent certification that no Israeli components are in a product exported to the Arab world.

The Arab boycott of Israel has also worked beyond being a boycott to destroy businesses in the United States and elsewhere just because a company has an office or conducts business in Israel, thus extending their economic war wherever possible. In September of 2003, a fake Nike advertisement started to circulate in Europe and the Middle East only to appear in the United States in February 2004. The fake ad spread slowly because it was so disgusting that few believed it was real.

The professional looking ad contains a photo of a blood covered Nike shoe and two Hassidic Jews in the background cleaning up a suicide bombing scene in Israel. The text within the photo reads, "You may not survive the blast, but your shoes will." The professional looking ad is an obvious fake and a sick joke. The email that the photo is attached to calls for a Nike boycott in protest of the ad, which is presumed by the senders to have been made by Nike, which it was not. Rest assured, the ad is a fake and is so disturbing that I did not publish it with my original story, as I did not want the graphic to be circulated. The quality of the photo here has been reduced and labeled as a fake to prevent further spreading of this sick joke.

When I contacted Nike, I learned that the photo originally appeared with a note claiming Nike is anti-Semitic for putting out the fake ad; however, the truth is this fake is one of many emails designed to get Jews upset at Jewish-owned companies or businesses with offices in Israel. The creators of the ad

Fake Nike Ad

want to trick Jews into boycotting companies on the Arab boycott list. Yes, Arabs want to get Jews to do their dirty work for them. In responding to the controversy, Nike stated the following: "This offensive ad was not authorized by Nike and has no affiliation with the company. It was obviously created by some individual who does not value human life and is seeking attention by leveraging our well-known brand name..." Nike is right. Making such ads takes a sick twisted mind, the kind of mind that wants to starve people out with an economic boycott, not to mention lobbing missiles into small towns filled with women and children, to murder indiscriminately. Make no mistake—the same mindset that does not value human life was involved in both the photo and terrorism.

Starbucks also, has been under continual attack, because its founder and CEO, Howard Shultz, is Jewish. While it is not uncommon for big businesses to come under fire because they are easy targets, some attacks against Starbucks have been specifically targeted at creating misinformation to get Jews to boycott Starbucks. Other campaigns have been waged at Starbucks for supporting U.S. troops in Iraq and Afghanistan. Starbucks has both company-owned and local independent operators, the latter of which mostly operate overseas. Starbucks was made available in Israel by Delek, a gas station company, but the venture proved unprofitable as Israelis just did not like the coffee and the partnership agreement was terminated. Soon after the closings, an email circulated claiming Starbucks closed the stores because "Neil" who was specifically named as the customer service representative and was proven not to even exist, reportedly stated Starbucks is an anti-Semitic company. Rather, Starbucks Chief Howard Shultz is a prominent and highly respected member of the Jewish community in Seattle, Washington where he lives; thus, this is a contemporary case of Arabs boycotting a company because it is run by a Jew.

There are independently owned Starbucks outlets throughout the Arab world, probably because Starbucks is, in my opinion, an addictive fad. Even still, many Arabs in the Middle East boycott Starbucks because Howard Shultz is Jewish. There have been several false emails meant to get Americans to not buy Starbucks coffee; these ads claim Starbucks is anti-American. As mentioned, Starbucks has been under fire for supposedly not supporting U.S. troops, which is completely false. If anything, Starbucks leads the corporate world with its donating of at least two 50,000 pound American Red Cross shipments of their coffee for U.S troops serving in Iraq and Afghanistan. I cannot name one company that has single handedly done more to make U.S. servicemen and women feel appreciated and connected to home, than Starbucks.

Another false rumor about Starbucks is that the company charged New York City firefighters for bottled water while they were rescuing people during the September 11 tragedy. This is simply not true. It goes without saying that firefighters have plenty of water and do not take latte breaks during house fires and other major disasters. Second, demanding or requesting free products is stealing, and as a former Red Cross volunteer and National Registry Emergency Medical Technician, I am very familiar with how these groups feed rescue workers in emergencies and rescue operations. Third, in many cases, police, firefighters, and emergency medical personnel are not allowed to accept any remuneration for their work in the line of duty. On the topic of the World Trade Center attack, we cannot forget that a fake bomb was placed in a San Francisco Starbucks store in 2006, and a real bomb was set off outside a Starbucks store in New York City in 2009. These bombing attacks were certainly not set out of love.

For the most part, the false claims against Starbucks, especially ones aimed at getting Jews not to buy Starbucks products, can all be traced back to the fact of Howard Shultz's religion. No other major company in recent history has been under fire the way Starbucks has for its connections to Jews and Israel, as if that were somehow in and of itself evil. If you still do not believe the attacks against Starbucks are based on anti-Semitism, then perhaps you should be aware that Islamic clerics have made claims that the Starbucks logo mermaid is the Jewish Queen Esther of the Purim holiday fame, who saved the Persian Jewish community from destruction. Therefore, according to those clerics, Starbucks is not only inherently Jewish, but it is also evil since it is glorifying the saving of Jews, an anti-Semitic claim that has been spread far beyond just the Islamic world.

The bizarre stories don't end there. In June of 2004, several Members of Congress told the U.S. Army they could not use Israeli bullets in Iraq after Muslims complained that American soldiers where shooting at Iraqis with Israeli bullets. Yes, the message which Muslims had a few Members of

Congress relay to the United States Army was that you can kill Muslims, but you can't insult them by using Israeli products. In fact, Jews serving in the U.S. Armed Forces in Iraq had to have Judaism removed as their religious preference on their U.S. Army issued ID cards. Sure, some may say it would be better to not list the Jewish soldiers' religion on the ID cards when going into areas hostile to Jews, but that should have been the soldier's choice, not a mandate. Just being an American in Iraq alone puts a person in a hostile environment, so specifically mandating the deleting of the Jewish religion from ID cards does not protect the soldier, but rather insults the soldier and Judaism. Jews have the right to be proud of being Jewish and nobody should demand Jews hide their own religious pride. Not listing the religion could be beneficial if the Jewish soldier were to be taken prisoner by the enemy, but why deny these soldiers their right to be identified as who they are, if they desire? Jewish soldiers were not going to be singled out or removed from their units as that would have destroyed unit cohesiveness; regardless, the Pentagon, for good or bad, did choose to remove the Jewish soldier's religious designation from there ID cards. These were not Israeli soldiers. These were U.S. soldiers. They were American soldiers who happened to be Jewish. Why did the Pentagon discriminate against Jews being able to identify themselves as they wished?

Perhaps the U.S. was trying to protect these soldiers beyond the call of duty. Perhaps the Pentagon did not want to offend Arabs or the Saudi Royal Family by openly having Jews protect Mecca and Medina, Islam's holist sites. Perhaps the Jewish soldiers needed the protection offered, by not having their religion listed on their ID cards. Perhaps the Pentagon went a little too far trying to do the right thing and ended up denying soldiers their pride of their religion. One thing for certain: it was done due to the levels of hatred in the Arab world toward Jews in general, not just Israelis or Israeli products. The underlying anti-Semitism in the Arab world is a key impediment to peace in the Middle East. Arab nations do not want Jews in their countries, even if the Jews are there to help them, and you cannot establish or even pretend to establish peace with those attitudes.

On November 6, 2009, with the help of Jerry Gordon and others, Major General Alfonsa (Al) Gilley, U.S. Army Retired delivered a speech to the B'nai Israel Synagogue, Pensacola, Florida for their Veterans Day Dinner. The topic was Jews who served in the U.S. military. After reading the amazing transcript, I invited Major General Gilley to appear as a guest on Jewish Community Radio, a show I host on WJCU[1], 88.7 FM, broadcasting from the campus of John Carroll University in University Heights, Ohio. On that show, which I archived at www.JewishCommunityRadio.org along with the Pensacola transcript, Major General Gilley completely dispelled the old anti-Semitic charge that Jews do not serve in the United States military.

Major General Gilley spoke about America patriots who served with distinction, including Haim Solomon, who financed the entire American Revolution. Mr. Solomon raised the money to feed and pay the soldiers who fought for American independence, including at synagogues. Then there is the story of Airman First Class John Lee Levitow, a Jewish Airman who suffered horrific injuries to save his aircraft when a magnesium flair ignited near on board ordinance. Major General Gilley also talked about Major General Rose, an unsung hero of World War II, amongst many others. Major General Gilley's words were so inspiring that I just could not end the show when I was supposed to, and I ran over by about fifteen minutes, a major no-no in radio. I thank Howard Regal for allowing me to cut into his time and especially WJCU General Manager Mark Kreiger for his understanding.

Far more Jews served in the United States military than Major General Gilley could have spoken about in the show or speech. Amongst many other Jews serving in our great nation, I know an Israeli who serves in the United States Special Forces. I also know United States Marine Reservist Josh Mandel, who volunteered for a tour of duty in Iraq while serving in the Ohio State House, and is now running for statewide office. These are but a few of the proud Jews who serve in the United State military, and they are all heroes. So, when you see a soldier in uniform, say thank you because that soldier may have already saved your life.

Currently, the U.S. Army has two contracts to supply the type of ammunition used in the M16 riffle, one from the Israel Military Industries Limited and the other from Winchester Ammunition. These two companies are best equipped to supply the Army with the needed ammunition; also, it is never smart to put all your eggs on one basket. Even still, neither company

---

can produce all the necessary ammunition alone. Both contracts are of equal value, $70 million each, and both companies supply high quality products. Considering that the United States is engaged in conflicts in both Iraq and Afghanistan, not to mention that Iran is a likely point of hostility, there is no way the U.S. can segregate ammunition or just use American-made ammunition in the Middle-East. It is just not practical or feasible. The Iraqi response is really the disturbing part. The complaint was not against United States soldiers using live ammunition to shoot at Iraqis—the complaint was that the bullets were made in Israel. They are essentially saying you can kill Muslims, but you can't insult them.

On that note, Israeli medications and medical devices are also banned in Arab countries, even if the device or medication is required to save someone's life. Perhaps this explains why so many Arab Sheiks visit the United States, especially the Cleveland Clinic, where they often receive lifesaving surgery from Jewish doctors. This, simply because these top doctors and medical advances are banned in Arab countries. There are actually two special royal suites at the Cleveland Clinic, paid for by the Saudi Royal Family, which is used as a private medical recovery facility within the hospital. I saw the two rooms a few years ago, and they are very plush. They hide as much of the standard medical equipment as possible to make the royal hospital visit as comfortable as possible, in a room that is more akin to a fancy hotel room than hospital quarters. The Saudis paid for it, illustrating hypocrisy within the Arab boycott, that certain elite secretly violate the boycott. The Saudi Royal Family and others just don't say anything to their subjects, because they are in power and can do whatever they want; thus, you can count on the Saudi Royals never telling anyone they have Jewish doctors and receive benefits of Israeli innovations. And they will certainly never mention that at least one Cleveland area hospital has its off-hour radiology scans interpreted in Israel; rest assured, the Saudis would never let that secret out to the Arab world. After all, what would the poor masses who live in squalor say when they find out their leadership, who insist in adhering to the Arab boycott of Israel, rely on Jews to keep them alive and healthy?

Adherence to the Arab boycott is apparently more valuable than the lives of children, as is evidenced by how the Israel boycotters would rather starve children to further their anti-Semitic cause. Born in the former U.S.S.R., Lev Leviev is a very successful jeweler who reportedly now lives in London and has a home in the United States. His New York City jewelry store has been the target of countless protests by divest-from-Israel activists, because he reportedly donates money to building schools in Judea and Samaria, among other causes. Mr. Leviev sees boycotts and protests in front of his New York City store not only because he does business in Israel, inherently making that a secondary boycott of Israel, the type of boycott the Office of Antiboycott compliance is directly concerned with, but also to intimidate others from wanting to do business in Israel. The boycotters and protesters are there to get media attention and send a message that doing business with or donating to projects in Israel will get you picketed and boycotted. Their goal is to block consumer purchases from businesses with any connection with Israel, even if the business has no presence in Israel. At the same time, the protesters are inherently supplying information about an illegal boycott activity, as well as encouraging a tertiary boycott, both of which clearly violate the U.S. Antiboycott laws.

In 2008, the United Nations International Children's Fund (UNICEF) broke its own charter by severing ties with Mr. Leviev, who was a major donor to UNICEF, simply because he also donated money to projects in Israel. In doing so, UNICEF decided to keep starving children hungry because it would rather see children starve than accept money from someone who builds schools in Israel. That is clearly a United Nations expression of hating Jews. The United Nations will gladly accept money for Jews as long as they comply with what the United Nations want them to do. Mr. Leviev does not live in Israel, so this is clearly an attack on Jews for their ties with Israel. The United Nations, where Israel is constantly under fire just for existing, therefore officially adopted the Arab boycott of Israel by virtue of a United Nations flagship subsidiary. The United Nations silence was an acceptance of the boycott of a member nation as official policy. The main point, of course, is that to the Israel boycotters, building a school, hospital or other humanitarian effort for Jews are grounds to justify starving children. This is clear anti-Semitism and the Leviev boycott is an extension of it.

Al Jazeera Television

This sick and perverted thinking was also evident when I debated divest-from-Israel leader Noura Erakat, the niece of Saeb Erekat, who is part of the terrorist Fatah-Revolutionary Council. Three years earlier, she stayed silent when sitting at the dais at the Israel hate-fest at Georgetown University, when people were screaming, "From the river to the sea," meaning push the Jews into the Mediterranean ocean to die and destroy Israel. This phrase remains a part of the terrorist Fateh platform, a subsidiary of the Palestinian Authority.

On Al-Jazeera Television, I challenged Ms. Erakat's false claim of Gaza being the victim of Israeli aggression, when Ms. Erakat blamed Israel for the Hamas terrorist rocket attacks on Southern Israel. This was reminiscent of Yasser Arafat, who routinely blamed Israel for the terrorist attacks that in fact he ordered on Israeli civilians. The technique of blaming the victim for being attacked is illogical at best, but more to the point it is an insult to morality. Unfortunately, blaming the victim is the norm in radical Islam, as is evidenced by the documented cases of women being punished for being raped, while the rapist goes free.

The primary topic of the debate on Al-Jazeera Television was the divest-from-Israel campaign, which she promotes and I am naturally against on grounds that it is anti-peace. Ms. Erakat's true essence came out when she complained about Israel's response to Hamas rocket attacks on Southern Israel. Her silence on Al-Jazeera, the same silence she had at Georgetown University, spoke volumes—Ms. Erakat refused to even acknowledge the Hamas rocket attacks existed, let alone were aimed at civilians. This ignorance clearly indicated she felt bombing Israelis was normal and justified. While some people try to place a moral equivalence to terrorism and the response to it, Ms. Erakat took that one step lower when she simply dismissed any and all negative claims regarding Hamas terrorism.

This was the drivel from the person who promotes the divest-from-Israel campaign, claiming the best way to achieve peace is to wage economic warfare, presumably by everyone who supports active terrorist engagements. That is what the divest-from-Israel campaign was designed for—to be the Palestinian Authority war machine outside of the Middle East. It is a vehicle of action for those who cannot engage in armed conflict against Israel.

I had planned to be very cordial in that appearance until just moments before we went live, when I discovered Al-Jazeera producers gave Ms. Erakat, who was in the Washington studios of Al-Jazeera Television, my entire pre-interview. As a result, Ms. Erakat opened with a rebuttal of my main points.

Although pre-interviews by television producers are normal, it is neither standard nor ethical to try to throw a guest under the bus by feeding your main points to the other guest. I must therefore conclude that Al-Jazeera wanted to throw me off guard, but I refused to play their game or be used as their political pawn. I had no alternative but to take Ms. Erakat out on facts, which I have plenty of, and argued very well. I proved Ms. Erakat was clearly against peace, advocated terrorism, justified terrorism, and promoted the divest-from-Israel campaign not as a means of promoting peace, but rather to promote her agenda of destroying Israel. That is exactly the purpose of the divest-from-Israel campaign—you cannot have peace with economic warfare with people who use economic warfare as an extension of terrorism. Real peace requires economic cooperation.

It is wrong to reward terrorists and terrorism with anything, especially a state, and in this case the attacks are from all sides: militarily, economically and politically. Just like continually rewarding a child for temper tantrums results in a spoiled adult who demands getting their way all through life, it is harmful to reward terrorism or even the threats of terrorism with concessions to stop people from screaming. It is the same thing. In civil societies we reward civil behavior, not tantrums. If you want to see two nations or even two neighbors living peacefully side by side, you have to display civility, not terrorism. If you just receive average customer service at a restaurant, you will leave a tip, but you will never leave a tip if treated badly. So I ask why in the world anyone would think rewarding terrorism with a state will do anything but send a message that terrorism, or bad customer service for that matter, is worth a thank you tip or statehood. Normal people believe in paying a fair price for goods and services you use every day and are against being ripped off. As such, the just compensation for peace is the reciprocation of peace and nothing more. The giving of anything more than an equal exchange, also known as concessions in the negotiation world, is wrong and only leads to demands for more concessions.

After all, if you can get something for nothing by throwing a tantrum, then why stop there? Israel has sent that message by entering into negotiations with terrorists, trading land for no peace, and releasing a massive number of murderous terrorists for single Israelis. While Judaism has the Mitzvah, or positive commandment, of the release of prisoners, Judaism also forbids the suicide, and the release of terrorist murderers has directly resulted in the direct murder of Jews in Israel.

As such, advocates of the divest-from-Israel campaign, which is essentially and by definition a boycott, are engaging in economic warfare and not the promotion of peace which they claim. They won't tell you that because it if they were honest, the advocates would inherently lose their arguments, which is why Ms. Erakat just ignored the tough questions I asked. She knew she could not truthfully admit her divest-from-Israel boycott campaign is about the destruction of Israel, the very points I had pinned her to the wall with while on Al-Jazeera Television.

A true peace initiative means building the infrastructure to work together, not tearing people apart and separating them as the campaigns of boycott and divestment promote. The goal of peace cannot be attained by treaties alone, which lack the underlying infrastructure to support the ink on paper. Peace treaties on paper may appear nice, but just like buying a car; you will crash if you don't learn how to drive first. Peace requires preparation, and that is what economic cooperation provides.

Land From Peace, Not For Peace

Just as with the Saudi Royal Family secretly accepting Jewish doctors when nobody is looking, there have been some breakdowns of the Arab boycott of Israel; however, this breakdown has been seen only in a few limited cases where in-vogue consumer fads or special technology needs become more important than the boycott. Coca Cola, for example, now has bottling plants in the Arab world, yet not without controversy. The Zionist Organization of America (ZOA) has been calling for a boycott of Coca Cola because of the way Coke products became available in Egypt. Coca Cola built a bottling plant on Jewish-owned land in Egypt without compensation to the exiled Jewish family that possesses the deed to the property. To paraphrase a ZOA press release, the Bigios family had owned land near Cairo since the early 1900s, though their land which was confiscated, or stolen, in 1964 during a campaign of anti-Semitism. In 1979, the Egyptian government ordered that the Bigios' property be returned, but the Egyptian courts would not enforce the order, according to the ZOA press release. Although the ruling verifies the Bigios land claim, the Coca-Cola Bottling Company of Egypt claims they purchased the land after it was privatized and now has clear title to the land; therefore, it feels that it does not owe anyone compensation. The Coca-Cola Bottling Company is aware of the claim and that the court has yet to act on the own ruling.

I believe Coca Cola wanted to act in good faith when they purchased the land. I also believe that Egypt took the opportunity to stick the Arab boycott in face of Jews by specifically steering Coca-Cola to buy the confiscated Jewish land, since the company not only has a presence in Israel, but also because the Coca-Cola Bottling Company is on the boycott list. Coke is an in-vogue product in Egypt, that most Egyptians still boycott; however, Coca-Cola is one of many international companies allowed to build in Arab countries due to their presence in other European countries, like France where anti-Semitism is rampant. Having a presence where anti-Semitism is practiced openly is the key to entrance in the Arab world. Just having a presence in Egypt does not mean Coca-Cola will be successful there, as the opposition to Coca-Cola is strong in the Arab world.

Despite the fact that Coca-Cola has received substantial documentation that the land they operate on was stolen, the Coca-Cola Bottling Company has refused to compensate the Bigios family for the land they are using, as part of their effort to open new markets and increase overall revenue. I believe Coca-Cola either did not perform a proper due diligence land title check, or the company received erroneous information from Egypt. Coca-Cola would be silly to give money to just anyone who has a claim to past land ownership, but in this case there is court documentation and the Coca-Cola Bottling Company knows the politics. It would be a good faith move for Coca-Cola to compensate the Bigios family, rather than enter a long-term battle which will cost Coca-Cola far more than a settlement with the Bigios family. This is not to say the ZOA is conducting a counter-boycott to the Arab boycott of Israel; rather, I believe this individual case presents itself as a reaction to attempts to counter the Arab boycott in Arab countries. Here, we see the irony of the Egyptian government's re-appropriation of stolen Jewish land in building a presence for a company on the Arab boycott list.

Egypt is one of several countries in which Jewish land has been confiscated in the name of anti-Semitism. Many Jews were exiled from Arab nations when Israel was declared and forced to flee only carrying what they could hold in their hands. The Arab nations would then confiscate their remaining land and goods. This was not just phenomena of the Arab-Israel conflict. As was the case with virtually every Jewish family under Nazi rule, my father's family farm land in Romania was also confiscated without compensation when the Nazis took over Europe. As stated earlier, the land Arabs want and claim for an independent Palestinian state is land purchased to create Israel; thus, we are seeing more of the same land grab as in the Bigios family case.

Kristallnacht II

In June of 2008, Syria changed one of it national laws regarding boycott enforcement by no longer requiring first-time patent applicants to submit declarations of compliance with the Arab boycott. At first glance, this sounds like a positive step towards the removal of the entire Arab boycott, but the reasons behind the move demonstrate how deeply ingrained the Israel boycott is within Arab society. First, by requiring its own citizens to comply with the boycott, the Syrian dictatorship demonstrated how much it fears Israeli products, and the high amount of energy the dictatorship exerts over the population to maintain the Arab boycott. Syria, the host country of the Central Boycott Office, wants to ensure its entire nation is in full compliance with the Arab boycott and wants everyone in the Arab world to know it. Second, the declaration requirement is meaningless in a country where compliance with the Israel blacklist is mandatory in all aspects of life. The new policy means Syria now allows its citizens to acquire patents based on copies of Israeli and Jewish technology in Syria, which the Arab world would accept, without the applicants having to lie by stating the items were not Israeli or Jewish in origin. It is an official Syrian license to steal from Jews.

These Syrian patents are just a way for Muslims to avoid lying, which would violate Islamic tenements; however, stealing from Jews is apparently justified, as that is exactly what loosening the boycott declaration requirement accomplished. Jewish and Israeli items cannot otherwise be patented in Syria. This legal change also facilitates the manufacture and copy of Israeli technologies in Arab nations under the approval of Syria. They put a Jew-free name on impostor Israeli products and technology under the Arab flag in order to sell technology in the pan-Arab world under the protection of the Syrian flag. It is a Syrian governmental license to steal and receive Arab versions of Israeli products into the open market.

One prominent organized Israel boycott/economic warfare campaign today is on the Internet with various Electronic Intifada websites. As the name clearly indicates, these are campaigns of war, not peace. By name alone, these websites, which promote the Arab boycott, negate all claims of peaceful efforts by the Arabs and their supporters who build and promote those sites. U.S. based, pro-Palestinian organizations tend to point to Electronic Intifada websites that are hosted in foreign countries, yet specifically target American audiences to avoid prosecution under U.S. Antiboycott laws. By relying on foreign-hosted websites, the Electronic Intifada promoters indicate the Arab world is completely aware of the Antiboycott laws and are actively working to circumvent those laws. These are the very same laws which were partially enacted to prevent foreign influence on and the creation of *de facto* U.S foreign policy. In fact, the boycott lists on those sites specifically target U.S companies under Jewish ownership and, again, Israeli academics. This is the equivalent of book burnings and the spray painting of "Jew" on store windows the way the Nazis did in Kristallnacht.

The following are examples of Americans intimidated from doing business with American companies under Jewish ownership:

- **Disney:** Yes, Mickey Mouse, whom the Arab world illegally copied for its official Palestinian Authority television station in children shows that promote the destruction of Israel and murder of Jews, is a part of the Arab boycott because Michael Eisner, a Jew, ran this publicly traded company. There is neither a Disney World in Israel nor any connection between Disney and Israel. The complaint, according to one hate-filled website, which I will not list because I refuse to promote hatred, is that: "Epcot Centre in Florida depects [their spelling, not mine] Jerusalem as the capital of Israel." Well, the fact is, Jerusalem is the capital of Israel. If that were a legitimate reason for a boycott, they may as well also boycott daylight because the sky is blue. Even with the divided Jerusalem proposal promoted by some, this irrational thinking clearly indicates the boycotters will never be satisfied unless Jerusalem is entirely under Arab control; however, that will never happen, once again proving the Arab boycott is about destroying Israel.

- **Home Depot:** This company does not have any stores in Israel, but again, it is run by a Jew, in this case Bernard Marcus, whom the Arab world terms as "an active Zionist." Here, they do not capitalize the word Zionist, as the boycotters do not recognize they legitimacy of Zionism because, well, it applies to Israel. To the hate-mongering boycotters, philosophy and thought are enough to earn a company boycott and blacklist status, which is again akin to book burnings as they feel any and all Zionistic and pro-Israel thought must cease. The Arabs promoting the Israel boycott are out to destroy any company with even a marginal connection to anyone who likes Israel.

- **Timberland:** I am not sure why I have to point this out, but as you have probably already guessed, the company is primarily owned by a Jew. The boycott stems from founder and CEO Jeffrey Swartz having visited Israel and then having the audacity to express his pro-Israel opinions there. Yes, just expressing a pro-Israel thought was enough to get Timberland boycotted.

- **Starbucks:** A pattern is emerging, if you have not yet figured. Yes, Howard Shultz, the founder and CEO of Starbucks, is Jewish. As previously stated, Starbucks didn't work in Israel, yet exists in the Arab world as independent outlets; however, most Arabs boycott the chain in North America, and there was an even a bombing in the United States because a Jew runs the company.

- **Sara Lee:** This is an example of a company boycotted not only because it has investments in Israel, but also because one of the executives received an award from Israeli Prime Minister Netanyahu. Yes, to the Arab boycotters, even a minor association with Israel is reason enough for a boycott despite this being an American company.

These are but a few examples of the many U.S. companies that Arabs boycott, strictly due to their Jewish relationships. In fact, just buying products from these companies makes a person *persona non-grata* in the Arab world. These secondary boycotts are even used as recruitment tools of the anti-Semitic campus campaign by not only giving students an action item to latch onto, but also by encouraging students to refuse to talk to their friends unless they too, refuse to buy Jewish, and not just Israeli products, so they too, can be a part of the little circle of hatred. Here the Arabs are encouraging intimidation of friends as part of their secondary boycott. Despite this not being expressly illegal according to U.S. Antiboycott laws, it is a form of secondary boycott and intimidation of businesses and consumers. The message is to comply with the Arab boycott or don't be my friend, which is at the very least disrespectful of the views of others and should never be tolerated.

There are thousands of businesses listed on various Israel boycott websites, and since these lists are primarily targeted to get Americans not to buy from these companies, you will see American companies listed because Americans tend to buy domestic. It is a tactic to give Israel boycott recruits something to feel good about. In some cases, however, you will see European sports teams boycotted, sometimes for the ownership and in some cases just because Yossi Benayoun, an Israeli soccer star, plays for a British team. Then there were the Iranian athletes who backed out of the Olympic competition because they did not want to compete against Israelis. Incredibly, the Iranian athletes were treated as heroes when they returned to Iran, not as the cowards they really are for refusing to compete against Jews. Perhaps the shame of possibly losing to a Jew would be a death sentence in Iran, a nation which has threatened to destroy Israel with nuclear weapons. The Olympics, of course, are meant to promote international brotherhood and peace, yet it was expressly boycotted because peace and reconciliation are not part of the Arab agenda. Iran is Persian, not Arab, but is signatory to the Arab boycott due to their shared hatred of Jews. Speaking of Israel in the Olympics, you should also know that the alphabetical parade of participating nations in the opening Olympic ceremonies must be modified at times because some Arab nations refuse to stand in line either immediately before or after Israel, once again demonstrating not a fear of but instead a hatred of Jews and Israel. It is not Israel that has refused their alphabetical position in line but Iran and Iraq.

You cannot foster peace under those conditions no matter what is written because paper agreements prescribing peace will never be respected unless all parties to that peace are respected. These fundamentals of peace require respect, and until Arab nations are willing to drop their fear of even standing near a Jew in a procession of nations, dreams of Middle-East peace can never be fulfilled.

The Cost to
Arab Nations

CHAPTER 4

Not only is the Arab Boycott of Israel hampering peace efforts, but it also hurts Arabs more far more than Israel. The Arab boycott causes inconveniences and added expenses for Israelis with their oil imports, but it is the Arab nations that spend considerable dollars enforcing their boycott. They spend their money looking under stones and inside computers to make sure they are free of Israeli components. It is sad the Kristallnacht attitude prevails in the Arab world, boycotting anything Jewish and going out of their way to make sure nothing Jewish exists in their lands. All the energy to enforce the boycott has a very expensive price in the Arab world.

The enforcement of the Arab boycott in the Middle East forces Israel to ship virtually all of its imports and exports, rather than drive them across a border in trucks, which adds cost to foreign trade. For the Arab world, just tracking the ships is expensive, as each ship must get permission from the CBO to enter Arab ports. While Jordan has some trade with Israel—the basis for a growing peace—every other Arab nation spends a considerable amount of money enforcing the boycott and maintaining their national boycott list. This even includes Egypt, which has a minimal tourism trade with Israel, a topic addressed in greater detail in Chapter 13: "From Boycott to Goldstone."

Virtually all Arab nations have disastrous economies. Despite having a large petrodollar economy—money is virtually being pumped from the ground—the most of the wealth in the Arab world is held by a relatively small number of individuals. The vast majorities in these nations live in complete squalor. That is not seen in the media because Arab kingdoms are not free nations; thus, they can restrict travel. This is especially true in Saudi Arabia where the kingdom forbids tourist visas and only allows foreign workers to be in designated areas. In addition to anti-free-market governments, the leaders of Arab nations, other than Jordan and Egypt, forbid any trade with Israel, meaning they are restricting their nation's from taking part in economic success. Just as in business where associating yourself with successful people makes you more successful; trading with successful business partners makes you successful as well. While Arab nations do trade with Europe and Western nations, their primary trading partner for decades had been the U.S.S.R., which was highly unsuccessful. The most successful neighboring trading partner for Arab nations is Israel, but that trade is mostly forbidden under the Arab boycott rules.

One of the best compendiums of the economic success of nations is the World Factbook published by United States Central Intelligence Agency. Besides spying, the CIA is responsible for gathering information about nations—all U.S. agencies use this information. The CIA World Factbook is publicly available on the www.CIA.gov website, and although available data sometimes vary by year from country to country, they do present a good comparative indication of the economic conditions globally. However, even with this data is not trustworthy, as dictatorships such as the Kingdom of Saudi Arabia only release what they want you to know; but, an examination of the numbers will reveal much of the untold story.

The following chart examines the Gross Domestic Product (GDP), or the overall annual measure of how profitable a country is. If you divide this number by the total population, you then get the average productivity of each individual, or the GDP Per Capita. Economists like to equalize this with currency exchange rates, to establish the absolute Purchasing Power Parity (PPP). By using the parity numbers, we can make fair comparisons to our own economy, thus helping us understand the actual living conditions in each country.

The GDP versus Per Capita in parity for 2006 chart (Sample data) per the CIA:

Country	GPP	PPP
U.S.A.	$13.06 trillion	$43,800
Israel	$170.3 billion	$26,800
Saudi Arabia	$371.5 billion	$13,800
Iran	$599.2 billion	$8,700
Egypt	$334.4 billion	$4,200
Syria	$78.04 billion	$4,100
Iraq	$87.9 billion	$1,900
Lebanon	$20.64 billion	$5,900
Jordan	$12.53 billion	$5,200

This chart is very revealing. The average Israeli has a much higher standard of living than those of their closest and most threatening Arab neighbors. The average Israeli has nearly double the income of the average person living in Saudi Arabia. When considering the ownership of durable goods, the average Israeli has an exponentially higher standard of living than the average Saudi resident, even though Saudi Arabia is touted as a major success and economic powerhouse in the Middle East. In Saudi Arabia, which has nearly half the PPP of Israeli, the Saudi Royal Family holds the vast majority of the nation's wealth. The Saudi Royal Family includes thousands of princes and princesses, all of whom spend their family share of petrodollar profits without ever having to work. Saudi Arabia has a population of about 27 million people, which includes roughly 5.5 million foreign nationals who work in high tech areas and are highly compensated for bringing in their expertise. This expertise is imported and rented, since the vast majority of those salaries are spent outside the Saudi Arabian Kingdom.

The foreign workers in Saudi Arabia are restricted regarding where they can travel, which falls in line with Saudi Arabian law forbidding tourism. This, because the Saudi's do not want foreigners to see and photograph their reported mass poverty. Islamic Haj pilgrims are restricted to being Muslim. Non-Muslims may not participate and the pilgrims may not travel freely. The mega-rich Saudi Royal Family prefers to hide and even deny the existence of their poor rather than solve their poverty problem, since it would take dollars from the national resource the Saudi citizens rightfully own away from the Royal Family. That also explains why the Saudi government does not publish the percentage of their population that lives below the poverty line. Foreign workers in Saudi Arabia tend to be unmarried engineers and other professionals recruited for their expertise. They usually have short-term contracts because the compensation is much higher than what they could make in the United States or elsewhere, thus justifying the hardships of not being with one's family for the contract's duration. Long-term contracts rarely exist because the Saudi kingdom does not want foreigners to become too comfortable in their nation. People who have accepted these contracts have told me they must observe Islamic modesty laws in public, yet have also attended wild private parties that include alcohol and other activities forbidden in Islamic law.

The high salaries for the foreign workers, which add into both the population and PPP numbers, coupled with the opulent lifestyle of the Saudi ruling class means there must be a very large percentage of people living below the poverty line. At base, the PPP in Saudi Arabia is about half of neighboring Israel and a third of the United States. There is a relatively small middle-class in Saudi Arabia, primarily consisting of the temporary foreign workers. These are to be considered optimistic numbers, because the official Saudi numbers cannot be trusted. Saudi Arabia is neither a free nation, nor does it have a free press; therefore, they can publish any numbers they want without scrutiny or audit, leading one to believe the reported numbers, as bad as they appear, are rather exaggerated and probably far worse. One good example of these numbers being fraudulent: the Kingdom boasts a 100% Muslim population, which cannot be true when considering the 25% foreign workforce that they count into their total population.

According to the foreign contractors I have spoken with, Saudi Arabia permits non-Islamic religious practice as long as it remains completely within the contractor's apartments; otherwise, non-Islamic religious practices are forbidden in public places. This also makes me wonder, especially considering the party reports, about the HIV/AIDS rate that the Kingdom fails to report; this is probably due to the fact that they are too embarrassed, since the Saudi Kingdom is an Islamic state and the Saudis fear Iran. The Saudis also feared Iraq under Saddam Hussein, which is why they allowed the United States to stage its attack against Iraq in the Saudi Kingdom. Of course, the Saudis later had to evict the United States military due to fears and threats both internally and externally for hosting the soldiers. It is likely that the Saudi fear of Iraq will return once the United States military relinquishes military rule there.

Egypt appears to be Israel's poorest neighbor with a PPP of $4,200. That works out to $16.15 for an average 8-hour day of work or about $2 per hour. However, people who make that little tend to work far more than forty hours a week—and that is an average. If you factor in the people working in cities, farms and industries, the poverty numbers in Egypt are astounding and scary at the same time. Perhaps this explains Egypt's net migration rate of -0.21 out of every 1000, meaning Egypt is hemorrhaging population as more people would rather move out of, than move into, Egypt, where most probably the more educated people seek a better living elsewhere. Considering how little money the average Egyptian makes, most Egyptians have to stay there, not because they fear losing money, but because they simply cannot afford to do anything more than engage in basic survival.

The same economic devastation exists in other Arab nations with similar PPP numbers. Contrast this with the Sudan, where the population is oppressed and murdered by its own government: the PPP in the Sudan is $2,200, or about half of Egypt, but in the Sudan there are aid organizations such as World Vision and UNICEF. You may recall that UNICEF rejected money from Lev Leviev, a Jew who grew up poor and engages in humanitarian efforts for all people including Muslims, a Jew whose money was rejected by UNICEF because he wanted to help Jews build houses and schools. Yes, UNICEF prefers to keep Muslims starving because a Jewish donor also donates to build houses in Israel. There is zero comparison to, or justification for, UNICEF's rejecting Mr. Leviev's money to save the lives of children. UNICEF just prefers the Arab boycott of Israel, the economic warfare that prevents peace in the Middle East, over children's lives. If UNICEF really wants to save children's lives, they would never reject Mr. Leviev's donations; rather, UNICEF is purposely perpetuating the problem that they are tasked and entrusted to solve by playing politics with the lives of children. That is criminal, and the criminal nature of engaging in economic warfare by the divest-from-Israel campaign as a cover story to bring peace to the Middle East.

Unquestionably, there are people in both the U.S. and Israel who are very rich and others who are impoverished; in order for a society to thrive, however, there must be a strong middle-class, the kind that exists in these two free market democracies. Strong middle-classes do not exist in radical nations like Saudi Arabia, which are more interested in population control and creating witch-hunts, than in building better lives for their citizens. Dictatorships tend to have small middle classes composed of people and the families of those who work in areas supporting the aristocracy, but that is usually it. Oppressed minorities are the hallmark of every dictator, because the fear and threat of being forced to live in squalor if one violates basic rules becomes a powerful motivator, which keeps subjects in line. Dictators have economic powers over their subjects, sustained by keeping the weak unable to resist and unable create any uprisings. Dictators who stay in power do so only by removing the means of popular uprising.

From an economics standpoint, free-market economies work far better than dictatorships, even with exorbitant oil profits. This is because no dictator can run an economy more efficiently than the basic rule of economics—supply and demand. Adding to their problems, the Arab boycott of Israel restricts the floundering Arab economies from successful Israeli investments. Israeli companies would love to take advantage of lower wages by building factories in Arab countries the same way U.S. companies build factories in Mexico to lower costs. Mexico benefits from U.S. investment, while Arab pride results in self-inflicted economic devastation.

On the other hand, Israel has some trade and a growing peace based on its growing trade, with Jordan. In fact, Jordan's economy has grown due to its trade with Israel. In 2006 and 2007, Jordan's PPP was $5,000 and grew to $5,200 in 2008, a 4% growth. Compare that with the PPP growth in the United States in the same period being less than 0.5% percent and Israel's growth in the same period as 2.5%. Jordan's economy is growing and that nation's standard of living growth is outpacing both that of the United States and Israel combined, due to Jordan's trade with Israel. This proves trade builds peace with mutual economic reliance and dependence; as a corollary, boycotts have the exact opposite affect.

The low PPP in Arab nations results from the single product economy—oil—and the limited internal economic growth because there is no middle class to buy or produce goods. It is not a matter of having a self-perpetuating bad economy, but rather the desire to maintain a peasant class of subjects instead of a productive and educated society that can overthrow the dictators. The Arab power structure has learned that an oil-price based U.S. recession hits them harder due to the Arab world's single-product economy; thus, they can never afford low oil sales. In the mean time, the goal of the Arab boycott is to destroy Israel economically, but in the end, the boycotting Arab nations are hurting themselves as they desperately need all the economic boosts they can get.

What the Arab world does not want the rest of the world to know is that the United States is on the verge of becoming a net-zero oil importer/exporter. If the United States were to open new oil fields, it would no longer need Persian Gulf oil, which would toss OPEC into a frenzy that would likely lead to its demise. Venezuela and Mexico would both panic, since those nations rely on oil sales to the United States to exist. Arab countries would be forced to trade with Israel to survive, thus creating the opportunities for peace.

Barring the dream of the collapse of OPEC, Israel, which has quickly become an industrial powerhouse, would benefit from the lower labor costs the Arab world would likely provide. It is the Arab world that would mostly benefit with trade with Israel, as evidenced by Jordan's blossoming economy. By developing a middle class, Arab citizens would have growing consumer buying power; thus, the overall economy of the Arab world would flourish. However, the Arab boycott of Israel prevents that and even perpetuates dictatorships by preventing the masses to rise from pestilence. The fact is that Israel, being the only free-market economy in the region, is exceedingly successful and quickly approaching the UK's PPP of $31,800. Considering the age differences between these countries, Israel is on pace to pass the PPP of world economic superpowers, including Australia and Canada, in the near future. Arab countries in the region, on the other hand, are in desperate need of economic boosts, yet they cling to this needless boycott like a radioactive trophy.

Simply stated, boycotts never foster peace because you cannot have peace with people you refuse to do business with, let alone share a pot of coffee. The egos of dictators prevent them giving up their economic stranglehold on their own economies because they feel they have everything they need, but as the Beatles so aptly sang, "Money can't buy (dictators) love." Rather, dictators worry all day about which army faction is plotting to overthrow them. These rulers seldom even trust their own wives, which is why they have so many—they engage in a never ending and futile search for a true confidant who can give undying love in return. As a result, they redirect their anger towards scapegoating others to justify their own shortcomings.

Apartheid Claims— There is No Parallel to Israel

CHAPTER 5

One of the most bantered about claims by the divest-from-Israel crowd is the charge that Israel is an apartheid state. That, of course, is an after-the-fact claim, since the Arab boycott of Israel preceded the apartheid claims by more than fifty years; thus, this cannot be a valid justification. Those who make that charge tend to use adjectives such as "evil" and "oppressive" to frame their argument. This technique distracts the audience into agreeing apartheid is evil while simultaneously blaming Israel for using such conduct. In an argument, Arabs and their supporters will discredit their opponents by asking questions like, "How can you say apartheid is not evil," as if everyone universally accepts Israel as being apartheid. This bait and switch tactic is meant to establish common ground with third-party listeners; it is a reference point for the Israel-bashers to direct their focus while recruiting people to their cause—fighting evil is always good so they falsely attach Israel to evil and change the focus of the argument. Arabs and their supporters use this misleading technique to catch Jews off-guard, which is why it is such a good recruiting tool.

This strategy is interesting, especially since the divest-from-Israel crowd knows they have a false claim, which is why they create the false frame around their argument. While some people see through that lie, there are those who believe anything just to help the underdog. These people believe the David verses Goliath image that the Palestinians falsely created and, as I will prove later in this text, the Palestinians neither have the intention of actually declaring a state, nor do they wish to achieve actual peace. The Palestinians are not the underdog: their campaign is in fact a Japanese Bunraku puppet show. Here, people maneuver stylized puppets with lots of makeup and elaborate costumes; the audience then ignores these people, despite their being clearly visible on stage. Just like in "The Wizard of Oz," Palestinians want you to "pay no attention to the man behind the curtain," or in this case, pay no attention to their destructive plans.

Others who get involved with the Arab boycott/divest-from-Israel crowd are looking for an excuse to express anti-Semitism, and they tend to grab onto the false Arab claim because it is an easy excuse. They scream evil in a crowded theater and create panic because nobody wants to be seen as the last person standing up for evil. Let's examine the facts starting with the definition of the word "apartheid".

This word has French and Dutch origins and means separate or apart. The policy of apartheid, which the South African government had openly practiced, was the law that decreed the separation of people based on race; however, it can also apply to the separation of people based on religion, ethnicity or other factors. Apartheid is the legally enforced separation of people based on discriminatory legislation, not discrimination by individuals. For the sake of argument, if we were to eliminate the state and discuss apartheid as discrimination by people alone, we would be disingenuous since the argument by the divest-from-Israel crowd is that Israel is an apartheid state, which did not apply that to individuals. Later in the text, I will discuss that a version of individual apartheid blame is now on the horizon. Some Israelis with diplomatic immunity are being charged with non-crimes in nations that are not part of the Arab-Israel conflict. Ironically, they are being charged for the sole purpose of creating a state the Palestinians do not even truly want.

Habeas corpus is a basic element of law and logic. Anyone presenting a claim must prove that claim. A classic example of how this can be abused is the question, "Do you still beat your wife?" This question starts off making an assumption of prior guilt and at the same time makes a current charge despite not having established any such events even occurred. These are also known as logically gratuitous statements, which are statements that, according to the rules of logic, can be equally denied. From a legal standpoint, charges must be proven before guilt can be declared. In courts of law, trials begin with the prosecution making their claim, not the defense. With some limited exception, the prosecution has the burden of proof and not the defense. In court, the defense attorney's job is to poke holes in the prosecution's case, which is all the defense must do to win. These points are important because it took about 20 years for the apartheid claim to finally gain traction on college campuses despite the claim having no basis in reality.

Groups that exist today, such as the General Union of Palestinian Students (GUPS), would banter around the apartheid claim, which is itself completely diversionary. It is meant to distract people from reality. While Arabs who have accepted Israeli citizenship have full voting rights and are even members of The Knesset, which is Israeli's Parliament, Jews are routinely denied these and other rights in Arab nations as prescribed by Islamic Sharia law. The Arabs are trying to refocus blame for their own human rights abuses onto Israel.

In the book *The Politically Incorrect Guide to Islam (and the Crusades)*, by Jihad Watch Director Robert Spencer, the author spells out how Islamic law prescribes the maltreatment of non-Muslims. In addition to requiring non-Muslims to pay special additional taxes when living in Islamic lands, Jews and women have no voting rights in the Islamic world. In Israel, all citizens, including Arabs and women, are allowed to vote. Under Islamic Sharia law, women have no say in anything and are treated as property. In Israel, like in all democracies, women have equal rights as their male counterparts. That begs the question: Where is the actual apartheid?

One thing the apartheid claimers do not want you to know is that in Israel's recent 2009 elections, Arab citizens of Israel voted for the United Arab List, which won four seats in the Knesset. Talab El-Sana, Masud Ganaim, Ibrahim Sarsur and Ahmad Tibi are clearly not Jewish names, and some Arab Members of Knesset have openly run for office with platforms calling for Israel's destruction. Can you imagine the controversy that would exist in the United States if someone were to run for Congress with the platform of destroying the United States? Along with concerns of constitutionality and treason, money would pour into the campaign of the opponent in the United States. Israel's open party voting system allows people to vote for a party nationally and the party slate wins seats in the Knesset based on the percentage of total national votes. So while there are no explicit Arab districts so to speak, Israel's system inherently facilitates a greater opportunity for Arabs, who are sworn to Israel's destruction, to partake in the government. This is also not the first time Arabs have been in the Knesset; at last report, there are currently 13 Arab members. In fact, there was even one Arab in Israel's very first Knesset. Since Jews cannot vote in Arab nations, this again begs the question, where is the actual apartheid?

In addition to Jews not being allowed in Arab governments, which are mostly dictatorships anyway, Jews are neither welcome nor safe in Arab countries. Jews were exiled from Arab nations such as Syria, Iraq and Jordan on the day that Israel was declared as an independent nation. As previously stated, Jewish identity is removed from the identification cards of American armed forces before deployment to Arab countries because Jews are not welcome there. Where is the actual apartheid?

There are also no separate rights or limitations within Israel for people based on race or religion, something the apartheid claimers want you to believe. Rather, Israel goes out of its way to ensure everyone has the right to practice their religion. In Jerusalem, for example, Israeli police are routinely given assignments guarding Christian and Islamic services. Where is the actual apartheid?

There is one item with merit to the apartheid claim, but it is mandated by U.S. brokered peace treaties. In Judea and Samaria, a.k.a. the West Bank, there are separate areas for Jews and Arabs. These lands are designated A, B, and C, at the request of the Palestinian Authority, which does not want Jews in areas they administered; however, Arabs are allowed in Israeli administered areas. In fact, the peace brokered deal mandates that Israel must allow Palestinian workers into Jewish areas while Israeli workers are not permitted within Palestinian areas. Where is the actual apartheid?

Are there checkpoints for Palestinians to cross into Israeli areas? Yes, and checkpoints exist at border points all around the world. Those checkpoints are what the Palestinian Authority wanted—the ability to cross into Jewish areas; thus, these complaints are ludicrous. Arabs, or anyone else for that matter, who trespass into Jewish areas in Judea and Samaria are directed away, like any trespasser would be anywhere else; however, on October 20, 2000, when two Israeli Army Reservists made a wrong turn into the Palestinian Police Compound in Ramallah, they were brutally murdered, just because they are Jews. The wife of one of the two murdered men reported she had happened to call her husband at the time and was gleefully told by one of the murderers," We are killing your husband." Afterwards, one of the lynchers, Aziz Salha, proudly displayed his blood-covered hands in a now famous photo while smiling in "victory." When Israeli Prime Minister Ariel Sharon stepped on the Temple Mount to pray, Palestinians responded with years of riots because the Arabs refused to tolerate any Jew even visiting areas they administer. The Arab world in general is completely intolerant of the religions of others. Again the question, where is the actual apartheid?

Documentarian Pierre Rehov has made several films depicting the intolerance of Palestinians toward Jews and Christians. One noted film is "Holy Land: Christians in Peril," which exposes how Palestinians desecrated and even set fires in the Church of the Holy Sepulchre during its siege. The church has been mostly silent about this incident and the Palestinian rulers, because it fears violent reprisal; its members participated in the making of the documentary anonymously in order to tell the world their story. In that film,

Mr. Rehov addresses what he calls "the hidden war against the Christians." In that and other films, Mr. Rehov interviews Christians in Bethlehem about their fleeing Bethlehem and other Arab cities out of fear and the dangers Christians face under Palestinian rule. Palestinian supporters will claim these were isolated incidents, though few actually make such statements, because they are blatantly false. The desecration of the church was done under the auspices of the Palestinian Authority, which had the complete police powers and ability to stop the desecration—but didn't. While the few Christians who remain in Bethlehem live in constant fear, Jews are not permitted entry. Again the question, where is the actual apartheid?

A recent example of the intolerance of Jews in Arab lands occurred when Israel granted Gaza semi-autonomy and evacuated Jewish settlers from the land. To help facilitate the creation of a Palestinian economic infrastructure, Jewish humanitarians and philanthropists, including Stephen Spielberg, spent tens of millions of dollars to purchase the existing Jewish agricultural infrastructure to jump-start the bleeding Arab economy in Gaza. Unfortunately, the response by the Palestinians was less than gracious. In the hours and days immediately following the Israeli pullout, every element of Jewish existence was destroyed. Palestinians destroyed millions of dollars of agricultural machinery and completely burned down all homes and synagogues. The Arabs in Gaza sought the complete obliteration of anything and everything Jewish, despite their destroying their own future prosperity in the process. The Jewish community in Gaza left behind a thriving business district, which was destroyed only because Jews had once owned it.

Some may claim that what happened in Gaza was similar to what occurred when Saddam Hussein was overthrown and Iraqis looted every government office and palace they could find. This is a poor comparison. In Gaza, everything was destroyed so there were no trace elements of any Jewish existence, yet the Iraqis kept items for themselves. The lesson from this is clear—the Palestinian hatred towards Jews is so strong that nothing connected to Jews is acceptable whatsoever. This explains why the Muslim Waqf, or council, had gone out of its way to destroy anything with a Jewish connection—and not just in Gaza. Despite Jewish objections, excavations under the Waqf-controlled Temple Mount in Jerusalem have persisted for several years. Here, the

Waqf used heavy equipment to remove all Jewish connections to Jerusalem and especially to the Jewish Holy Temple site.

The 1993 Oslo Accords were a failure. Officially termed the Declaration of Principles on Interim Self-Government Arrangements, the Oslo agreement was meant to eventually result in "final status" negotiations between Israel and the Palestinians. It was doomed from the beginning, because there was no consideration for how to sustain those borders. The Oslo Accords did, however, successfully create border lines that separate Jews from Palestinians, borders Israel did not want but was forced to accept under international pressure. These same lines are now used to blame Israel for the nonexistent apartheid, since Israel does not administer the land where apartheid allegedly occurs.

Soon after the Oslo Accords were signed, the Palestinians took administrative control over the ancient Jewish alter site found on Mount Eyval, which is in the Bible[1]. They completely obliterated all traces of it to eliminate evidence of Jewish history in the land. At the same time, the Palestinians gained control of Jacob's Tomb, which is in Shechem/Nablus, and they began to destroy it to build a mosque on that site; fortunately, international outrage forced them to stop. While Jacob's Tomb is a minor holy site in Judaism, the intention of building a mosque on the site was to forever hide its location, thus further demonstrating the complete lack of respect that Arabs have for Jewish antiquities. Israel, on the other hand, has laws in place that protect religious holy sites, including Muslim holy sites. Again, the question is where is the actual apartheid?

Let's face it. Jews are not welcome in Arab areas while Arabs, who have citizenship in Israel, have full voting rights. The apartheid claims by those promoting economic warfare with the divest-from-Israel campaign and boycott, use the apartheid claim to obfuscate their own hatred of Jews. Arabs just don't want Jews anywhere near them. Making blatantly false and disparaging statements to push one's own failings specifically upon Jews and Israel, is anti-Semitic and reminiscent of Nazi Germany. The false apartheid claims are certainly not made out of love, yet the Palestinians and their supporters want you to think that they love Jews, but hate Zionists. That is a false claim:

1.Deuteronomy 11:26-29

just as you cannot separate the Pope from Catholicism, you cannot separate Israel from Judaism. Being anti-Pope is being anti-Catholic and being anti-Israel is thus, the same as being anti-Semitic. Israel and especially Jerusalem are central to Judaism—they are inseparable.

One of the problems in Gaza and with the Palestinian Authority is that the leadership has stripped the residents of all hope of achieving anything better on their own. By constantly telling their constituents everything is Israel's fault, the Arabs believe that lie the same way Hitler blamed Jews for all of Germany's problems before World War II. The fact is, Gaza is in a parallel state of existence with pre-WWII Germany—both have economies in shambles, with Jews being the scapegoats. Today we are in a prolonged Kristallnacht, as people around the world boycott Jewish businesses rather than just one country. Additionally, the equivalent of Nazi book burning is the modern Arab academic boycott of Israel, which accomplished the same thing the Nazis desired—the banning of Jewish ideas only because Jews had thought of them.

Meanwhile, when Jews and Christians from all over the world visit Jerusalem, a common tourist destination is the Arab market, or Shuk, where price haggling is practically a sport. The reason Jewish and Christian tourists shop there is simple—they are sending a message that they want peace and cooperation with Arabs. Unfortunately, the returned response is Arabs' boycotting Israel, and Jews in general, with an occasional false complaint that Israel is using apartheid methods. Arabs are more than happy to take money from Jews, as they do with oil and aid, yet do not respond with business or even peaceful relations in kind. Israel buys Arab oil on the open market after first being offloaded in Europe and reloaded for shipment to Israel, thereby indicating the Arab dictators will take indirect dollars from Israel to support their lavish lifestyle while their royal subjects live in poverty, but accept neither Israeli currency nor reciprocal trade.

It is like a science fiction movie plot or a slapstick comedy routine, because the Arab boycott began long before the apartheid claim, despite some individuals wanting to change history by saying apartheid justifies the boycott. It is not even a case of cause and effect, or the ends justifying the means. The Arab world knows the apartheid claims are blatantly false, yet they mask this by calling for a global boycott upon Israel as if their boycott had never existed before.

Suddenly in late 2009, the Palestinians Authority attempted to play the part of a magician with a smoke screen game. They announced "Abracadabra! Boycott Israel! You never saw this before. It's new. Trust us!" The Palestinian Authority, of course, has been at the forefront of the boycott Israel campaign, so the sudden and independent announcement calling for a boycott of Israel was nothing more than an attempt at getting publicity, which worked in the short run because they received media attention.

The effects of the boycott, in response to apartheid, are rather curious. A successful boycott requires a stated objective with a plan to achieve that goal. The Arab goal is, of course, the complete destruction of Israel, but that is not what they tell the people they recruit. When the boycott of South African products was declared in response to actual apartheid, the goal was to pressure the South African government to end their discriminatory government where a minority wealthy white class ruled over a starving working class black majority.

By using the apartheid claim, the Palestinians are telling the world they want to end apartheid in Israel so they too, can have justice, but the purposed, complete destruction of every remnant of Jewish life in Gaza reveals the truth—the Palestinian goal is clearly and unequivocally the complete destruction and obliteration of Israel and the Jewish existence. This is not conjecture. The Palestinians have demonstrated their goals by destroying all evidence of Jewish history, and for that matter Judaism itself, with their intolerance of Jewish thought and ideas as seen by the academic boycott of Israel and of anything related to Jews.

The main problem resulting from the South Africa boycott is that the result was wide-scale job losses amongst the poor black majority population. Because the poor people had less money, there was an alarming increase in starvation. The ruling class minority white population was not financially affected significantly because the majority black community was suddenly willing to work for less money to survive, which for the ruling class meant inherent compensation for any boycott-related losses. In other words, the people the South African boycott was intending to help were the ones to suffer the most, which is often the irony of such boycotts.

A similar situation exists with the Arab boycott. Gaza, for example, does not benefit from it in any manner. Gaza did not benefit from the destruction of its infrastructure, which otherwise would have created income by exporting crops to Arab nations or European countries. To be successful in business, you must associate yourself with successful business people; however, the Arab boycott is hurting the Palestinians while Israel has found other trading partners and does not rely on Palestinian trade. To make matters worse for the Palestinian financial future, which lacks a prosperous trading partner, Saudi Arabia and Iran are pumping millions of dollars into Gaza, the world sends the tons of humanitarian aid that enters Gaza daily through Israel, and Israel still supplies Gaza with basic utilities. As a result, Gaza has become a charity basket that offers very little in the nature of exports or trade. The Arab world knows this and wants to perpetuate it as a political tool against Israel. As long as Gaza is poor, Israel can be blamed. This explains why Jewish farm property in Gaza was destroyed—being successful in business would destroy the Gaza reliance on foreign money and thus influence.

Not only is Gaza fully dependent on other nations, but also the Arab world does not want Gaza to be independent. As an independent entity, the Arabs in Gaza would suddenly have to run their government and people would have to hold real jobs. This change would completely take away their time to design, build and indiscriminately launch rockets to Israel, which is why the Arab world is happy with the status quo.

The apartheid claim and all of its manifestations prove that the Arab boycott of Israel is the single biggest impediment to peace in the Middle East, since you cannot have peace with anyone who will not sit down with you even for a cup of coffee. Israel is relatively prosperous even without open trade with the Palestinians and most other Arab nations. While Israel would benefit from that open trade with its enemies, the Arab world would benefit far more. The false apartheid claim is just an added layer to preventing trade, the opposite direction of what needs to be accomplished for a true road to peace, as opposed to previous failed policies and meaningless Nobel Peace Prizes.

In early January of 2009, through peace envoy Senator George Mitchell, President Obama launched a trial balloon threatening to withhold load guarantees and economic aid to Israel. The money Israel receives is part of the Camp David Accords, which also bribes Egypt with substantial aid as a way of promoting peace. By unilaterally blocking one side, the United States would both be violating the Camp David accords, which fostered some peace with Israel, and joining the Arab efforts to isolate Israel economically.

Soon after, that trial balloon was retracted. Several days later, Secretary of State Hillary Clinton announced she wanted to see an immediate restart of peace talks based on Israel negotiating away Jerusalem. In his first State of the Union Address delivered on January 27, 2010, President Obama said we must "reform export controls consistent with national security." The line was so vague it got little applause or media notice. While he was hopefully only speaking about expanding exports to new markets, the term export controls has a specific legal definition. It refers to laws that ensure American-made goods that may be used for military purposes do not end up in the hands of nations that may use those goods against the U.S. and its allies. In relation to the Arab boycott and Middle East peace, reforming export controls also may refer to the U.S. Antiboycott laws and policies to enforce it. The timing is worrisome because that line can easily be interpreted as using export control policies to coerce Israel to accept a Palestinian state without first creating the infrastructure to sustain peace, thus dooming the process to failure.

This, of course, is post-justification of President Obama's Nobel Peace Prize, without addressing the root and sustaining issues needed for a lasting peace in the Middle East. Land for peace has always failed:

- Jordan was created on May 25, 1946, stemming from the British modification of League of Nations mandate. 75% of the land that was meant to go entirely to Israel was instead cut out to create an Arab Palestinian State. The idea was to end all land disputes by separating Jews from Arabs and creating a final land status. This was the original land for peace deal. The Arab world reneged on that final status agreement when the Arabs jointly attacked Israel on its Independence

Day, May 14, 1948. Despite the Arabs agreeing to the original land for peace deal, the very first land for peace deal failed and proved the Arab world does not want Israel to exist whatsoever.

- Israel captured the Sinai Desert in 1956 during a war the Arabs started. Then in the 1978 Camp David Accords with American President Carter, Israeli Prime Minister Begin and Egyptian President Sadat, Israel agreed to remove all Jewish settlements in the Sinai Peninsula and return the land to Egypt. The only reason Egypt and Israel have not been to war is that Egypt relies on the U.S. economic aid as part of the Camp David Accords to survive. As proven in Chapter Four, Egypt is broke and cannot afford to feed its people, let alone engage in war with Israel. Jews were thrown out of their homes in the Sinai by Israel for the promise of peace, which barely exists today. The United States has to bribe Egypt in the form of foreign aid not to attack Israel, so there is no peace for the sake of peace. Egyptian economic success, which is not on the horizon, would not create a threat to Israel. Israel would be safer and perhaps even oil independent had it not been for the Camp David Accords; thus, the Sinai Peninsula land for peace deal failed.

- The establishment of Palestinian Authority control in Judea and Samaria by the Oslo Accords utterly failed, as proven by persistent terrorism. In that agreement, the Palestinian Authority was legally bound to put an end to terrorism, which the Palestinian Authority has not only failed to do, but has rather encouraged and facilitated. In response, Israel built a barrier to prevent terrorism, resulting in unfair criticism and phony war-crimes charges stemming from Israel fulfilling the primary mission of every nation—defending its own citizens. The Oslo Accords were centered on a promise for peace, and it failed.

- Israel's unilateral evacuation of Gaza was meant to give the Palestinians everything they wanted—a land with no Jews. Palestinians had used the presence of Jews as the reason for their terrorism, yet Gaza terrorism and violence persists even without a Jewish presence. Israel's leaving Gaza was meant to foster peace, but failed miserably.

Had land for peace been what the Arab world really wanted, the Arab-Israeli conflict we see today would not exist, as shown by peace having failed to occur in every Israeli land for peace effort. Israel has always been the one to give away land and make concessions for little to nothing in return. There is no reason to believe that giving any additional part of Jerusalem to the Palestinians, who already control East Jerusalem and the Temple Mount, will result in any peace.

Benjamin Franklin said, "The definition of insanity is doing the same thing over and over and expecting different results." That is what the Obama Administration is doing—pressing another land for peace deal, a formula which has always failed. The Arabs want more concessions from Israel, knowing full well that nothing will come from them other than the justification for President Obama's Nobel Peace Prize and a personal ego boost for President Obama. Had land for peace actually been a working formula, we would have had peace in that region long ago. When this plan inevitably fails, the Obama administration will surely blame third parties for the failure, the same way every administration has done in the past.

The Obama Administration is following the false apartheid claim logic, which itself cannot succeed because it is based on a complete fabrication. Even if another land for peace deal were to be implemented, it would not end the false apartheid claim that is continually showered on Israel. As evidenced by articles claiming to be from the "occupied Gaza Strip" despite no Jews being there, Palestinians and their supporters still blame all their personal woes on Israel. Israel cannot possibly be considered an occupying force in Gaza, since Israel is not there. Claims against Israel, including the apartheid claim, are illogical, but persist because the Palestinian goal is not peace with Israel, but instead permanent vilification of Israel until there is no more Israel.

This situation alone demonstrates the need to clearly reject the apartheid claim and its manifestations. The apartheid claim against Israel is nothing more than a rouse to distract the world from the actual Arab goal of the destruction of Israel. Do not fall for it. Hitler taught the world that the more you repeat a lie, the more people will believe it, which is exactly what is happening with the false apartheid claim. Moral people have the inherent obligation to reject the false apartheid claim outright and to teach those who propagate it of its dangers.

Origins of and the Present Day Divest-from-Israel/ Boycott Campaign

CHAPTER 6

The Palestinian Liberation Organization, or the PLO, was established in 1964, sixteen years after Israel was established. The PLO's singular goal was the destruction of Israel through terrorism, thereby augmenting the stated greater Arab plan of literally pushing the Jews into the sea. To this day, shouts of "from the river to the sea" can be heard at pro-Palestinian rallies. The PLO was essentially the Fateh terrorist group attempting to become an umbrella group of about ten smaller Palestinian terrorist groups, all of which shared the same goal of destroying Israel. Full unification never materialized, due to internal power struggles, and even today the Palestinian Authority cannot control Hamas, which rules in Gaza; however, the PLO did manage to ensconce itself as the primary voice for the Palestinian Arabs despite no internal elections or selection process. Much to the chagrin of other terrorist groups, the United States unilaterally created their artificial, yet officially recognized, world leadership function in an attempt to advance peace efforts. Originally run by arch-terrorist Yasser Arafat, the PLO was responsible for hundreds of terrorist attacks resulting in the murders of women and children, hijacking and bombing of aircrafts, and even the terrorist attack in the Munich Olympics.

Some people have argued that the Palestinians who live under PA rule do not all agree with the underlying PA philosophy. That is not the case. Palestinians who completely agree with the Palestinian Authority and Hamas have emigrated from the PA areas to Europe and the United States, which in turn clearly indicates two vital points. First, the image projected by calling Palestinians "refugees" is a misnomer, because they are not locked in camps; rather, they are free to hold jobs, build houses, and even move out of those areas. Second, by virtue of the fact that those living in PA—and Hamas-controlled areas have effectively chosen to reside there, they have personally accepted the destruction of Israel as their personal primary focus since this is the primary focus of both the PA and Hamas. There is no getting around that fact. The people who live there want to live there and accept its political realities. If you look at the website of the Middle East Media and Research Institute[1], you will see official Palestinian Authority television broadcasts, not just comments by Islamic clerics, calling for Israel's destruction. This confirms the fact that the Palestinian Authority endorses the message of the total destruction of Israel despite contradictory claims to seek peace. If the Palestinians truly want peace with, and alongside of, Israel, one has to wonder why the official Palestinian media does not broadcast that message instead.

As an outgrowth of the PLO, the United States established the Palestinian Authority in 1994 as part of the Oslo Accords. It became the political arm of the PLO, with the intent of transforming the terrorist organization into a governmental body. Sixteen years later, the terrorist attacks continue, which

1.www.MEMRI.org

is a major reason why no Palestinian state has emerged despite two offers by Israel to create an independent Palestinian state during the Oslo Accords negotiations. Israel's Member of Knesset and Cabinet Minister Benyamin Begin, a liberal in the Likud party, offered reasons as to why no Palestinian state has been created. When speaking in Cleveland, Ohio in September 2009, Minister Begin stated he feels the PA never created a state because "they do not want one." Minister Begin may very well be right considering the divest-from-Israel campaign and continued violence against Jews and Israelis in that region.

The PLO became a convenient tool for the Arab nations. Recognizing the failure of the 1973 Yom Kippur war, the Arab world realized they would not be able to destroy Israel militarily and had to utilize other methods. In 1974, the Arab nations directly supported the PLO, which was acting as a non-governmental or even trans-governmental entity, thus making it a perfect tool for the Arab world to use to attack Israel, while separating itself from any direct blame or consequence. This separation created a plausible denial shelter, as Arab nations could neither financially afford another military decimation by Israel nor handle any internal political fallout resulting from another military loss. Funding the PLO and terrorism helped Arab nations weaken Israel's morale, while the Arab countries rebuilt their military and national infrastructures. Terrorism proved so effective, as evidenced by Israel eventually having to violate its own policy of never negotiating with terrorists with concession after concession, that terrorism flourished and continued to work. Israeli negotiations and concessions with terrorists sent the message that the more terror the Palestinians inflict on Israel, the more the Palestinians will get in return. By rewarding bad behavior, Israel both encouraged and got more of it.

The PLO did not operate in a bubble. Undoubtedly with the help and support of the Arab nations, all of which were signatory to the Arab boycott of Israel, it developed a three-phase plan as official policy.

1. Through the "armed struggle"[2] to establish an "independent combatant national authority" over any territory that is to be "liberated" from Israeli rule.[3]

2.read that as terrorism, an important point in Chapter 9, Campuses Today
3.Article 2 of the PLO Charter

2. To continue the struggle against Israel, using an interim Palestinian state as a base of operations.[4]

3. To provoke an all-out war in which Israel's Arab neighbors destroy Israel entirely[5].[6]

Phase One is the establishment of an interim Palestinian state by means of terrorism; Phase Two is to use this Palestinian state to attack and weaken Israel; and Phase Three is the total destruction of Israel as a pan-Arab victory. If you think some of this sounds familiar today, you are correct. Although not declared as a state, Gaza functions as an independent nation from which cities in Southern Israel such as S'derot, face constant rocket attacks. Meanwhile, Hezbollah currently controls Southern Lebanon, and rocket fire into Northern Israel has resumed despite Israel's clearing of the areas under Prime Minister Ehud Olmert. Israel was able to thwart attacks to Central Israel against most Palestinian terrorist attacks due to the necessary, yet highly criticized defensive wall.

Instead of being under fire by Arab nations, Israel is under fire from non-nations with undeclared armies, or in other words terrorists, who in many cases build improvised weapons and specialize in rocket and mortar attacks.

On the topic of Israel's response to terrorism, Israel faces a worldwide double standard. While some Americans criticize the United States for being in Iraq after the World Trade Center attack, by saying the United States should only be fighting in Afghanistan, Israel is regularly criticized for any response to terrorism. That is tantamount to saying Israel does not have the right to defend itself, which is absurd. Israel is the only country in the world to face such charges, and various organizations have passed resolutions recognizing Israel's right to self-defense.

Implementation of the three-phase plan started with introducing the idea of an independent Palestinian state to the world. To achieve this with its three-phase plan, the PLO pushed the concept of an independent Palestine on campuses where young minds are still impressionable. Because most young people

---

4. Article 4 of the PLO Charter
5. meaning to liberate all Palestinian territory; the word "entirely" also means killing all Jews there
6. Article 8 of the PLO Charter

these days are not deeply interested in politics or history, these distractive campaigns inherently become easier to push and therefore take hold.

The PLO itself did not officially operate in the United States to conduct public relations campaigns. Instead, groups such as the General Union of Palestinian Students (GUPS) pushed the concept of creating an independent Palestine or, as they claimed, "the liberation of Palestine." Of course we must not forget that there never was a state of Palestine, so there was/is no state to be liberated. If that campaign were to have been a television commercial selling a retail product, it would have been the classic and illegal bait and switch campaign. Still, the Palestinian bait and switch persisted.

Many viewed the GUPS and other similar campus groups as supporting the blood-thirsty terrorists until President Clinton suddenly granted credibility and legitimacy to terrorist supporters by helping create the Palestinian Authority in 1995. This gave Palestinian groups an officially recognized and acceptable political entity to associate with, rather than terrorists. Of course, only the names had changed and not the anti-Semitic rhetoric and policies, such as the complete destruction of Israel; those still remain. And, as we see with the Arab boycott of Israel to which the PA is signatory, this group still wishes to punish Jews and anyone associated with Jews for having any business or academic connections.

The Oslo Accords did force one change to the three-phase plan. By agreeing to establish a final border state, the Palestinian Authority essentially agreed to not act upon stage two or three of their three-phase plan. In the negotiations, the Palestinian Authority agreed to "final status negotiations," meaning the Palestinians were bound by agreements not to destroy Israel and that any state they would agree to would constitute a final border agreement. In the process, the Palestinian Authority itself removed the wording declaring the destruction of Israel from their constitution; however, it allowed all subsidiaries, including Hamas and its very own Fateh, to retain all wording and vows to destroy Israel in their constitutions. In other words, the Palestinian Authority still recognizes the destruction of Israel as central to its mission—it just allows its subsidiary organizations to do the dirty work. By permitting all Palestinian Authority subsidiaries to retain the stated goal as the complete destruction of Israel, the Palestinian Authority is both respecting and approving the fact that it is the umbrella organization of an association calling for the annihilation of Israel. Nothing has changed from the PA's original policies and stated goals for Israeli genocide.

From a practical standpoint, by agreeing to the idea of a final status negotiation, the Palestinian Authority had changed the way it had to operate publicly, which may have been a planned public relations move. First, as was previously stated, final status negotiations means the establishment of a final, not interim, Palestinian state alongside Israel, not in place of Israel. That presented a dilemma for the Palestinian leadership, which attempted to placate everyone. On one hand, they presented themselves as peacemakers to the world, yet when speaking to his fellow Palestinians, Yasser Arafat would scream "Jihad, Jihad, Jihad" without any outcry. That call to war is not unique. MEMRI, the Middle East Media and Research Institute,[7] constantly exposes and posts videos with English translations of various Islamic clerics and Palestinian political leaders as they address crowds calling for the obliteration of Israel.

Second and most importantly from an Islamic religious standpoint, the Palestinian Authority can neither change its stance toward the complete destruction of Israel nor recognize Israel's right to exist. Accepting the existence of Israel contradicts the idea that all of Israel is Dar Al-Islam, or land that was once under Islamic law and therefore must always be under Muslim rule. Acceptance of Israel and its right to exist by Palestinian leadership would therefore constitute political suicide, and so far no Palestinian leader has been brave enough to make that move, but I feel it is possible to achieve real peace. The best way to achieve that recognition is through the slow building of trade, as was the case with Israel and Jordan. The more nations rely on each other as trading partners, the higher the cost of war and thus incentive to sustain peace.

This also correlates to why Gaza, which does control its own borders, has not been declared as a state—such a declaration would negate claims to any other land for statehood because the PA agreed to create a final status state within the Oslo Accords. If the Palestinians did consider the Oslo Accords a public relations maneuver, it certainly backfired.

---

7. www.memri.org

President Clinton touted the Oslo Accords as a win-win for everyone because (1) Israel no longer had to administer a hostile Palestinian constituency that could have eventually become Israeli citizens, should Israel annex Judea and Samaria and (2) the Palestinians were put on the path to statehood. However, it was really a lose-lose, since Israel left the final status of Jerusalem, which is not negotiable by any Israeli government, dangling as a carrot in the wind. Perhaps Minister Benjamin Begin is correct when he said the Palestinians do not want peace, but either way, Oslo is an inherent failure from inception and yet again proves that land for peace does not work; it has simply never worked anywhere in the history of the world.

Saudi Arabia had recognized the inherent failure of the Oslo plan, which is why it proposed an alternative peace plan in 2002. This plan would move Israel to the 1967 "Auschwitz borders," aptly named, because it would have given Israel a seven-mile wide corridor between a militarized Palestinian state and the Mediterranean ocean, thereby placing Tel Aviv in Katyusha rocket range from the proposed Palestinian state. These borders would put all of Israel at the imminent verge of destruction, thus the name "Auschwitz borders." Israel is a very small country and its borders are important for security purposes. The Palestinians know they cannot get the Auschwitz borders they want, which would have facilitated their three-phase plan, hence the public relations benefit for settling on the Oslo plan. The Palestinian negotiators only later realized how the Oslo plan ruined their three-phase plan, which is why Saudi Arabia proposed a plan to completely negate the Oslo Agreement. Knowing Israel would reject the plan, the Saudis knew that simply floating the idea would make Israel look bad for rejecting a peace plan. It was a chess game move with no real intention of physical success, just public relations success.

The Kingdom of Saudi Arabia, as you may recall, is not only signatory to the Arab boycott of Israel, but it also forbade the U.S. Army Corps of Engineers from hiring Jews to work in their dictatorship. The Saudi Arabian kingdom also sends stipends to the families of suicide terrorists for sending their children to be "martyrs" by strapping bombs across their bodies and murdering Israeli civilians. This encourages war, not peace. Saudi Arabia is neither Israel's friend nor a friend to Jews anywhere in the world, as proved by its own official boycott list. That Saudi plan was clearly meant to destroy Israel.

With Oslo, the three-phase plan needed to be updated. Suddenly in 1987, in walked in an American law professor who, as an advisor for the creation of a state, gave the Palestine Liberation Organization exactly what it needed to maintain its efforts to destroy Israel, while keeping the overall integrity of the three-phase plan. University of Illinois law professor Francis A. Boyle is perhaps the key American player for the Palestinians, and he managed to keep himself out of the Middle East spotlight despite becoming a key consultant to the Palestinian Authority. When he finally took credit for his work, few took notice. In his articles, he managed to not only demonstrate his affinity for the creation of a Palestinian state, but also validate rumors of his being anti-Semitic.

In a January 2002 article titled "Law and Disorder in the Middle East," which was published by Americans for Middle East Understanding[8], a group dedicated to Israel-bashing, Professor Boyle discussed his direct involvement as a consultant to the Palestinians in negotiations for peace. Boyle states that he advised the Palestinian negotiators to reject Israel's proposals to create a Palestinian state, and that the Palestinian negotiators took his advice "after consultations among themselves, and under the chairmanship of Dr. Abdel Shafi." Afterwards, Palestinian negotiator Dr. Abdel Shafi practically gave Professor Boyle carte blanche to write a counterproposal to Israel's offer of a Palestinian state. To ease the concerns of Dr. Shafi, Professor Boyle said, "As you know, I was the one who first called for the creation of the Palestinian state back at United Nations Headquarters in June of 1987, and then served as the legal adviser to the PLO on its creation. I will do nothing to harm it!"

This statement is very telling, not so much for his being the first person to call for a Palestinian state, but because he had served as a legal advisor to the terrorist Palestine Liberation Organization. Professor Boyle was, therefore, the world stage lawyer for the world's worst and largest terrorist organization and defender of terrorist actions. Let us not forget that the provisions of the PLO charter call for the complete destruction of Israel, and for Yasser Arafat's stated goals of pushing the Jews into the sea. These are not statements of either support or indifference to Jews; rather, such support is meant to remove all Jews from the Middle East by means of an "armed struggle," which is the

8. http://www.ameu.org

wording the PLO uses to propagandize its terrorism. Boyle's own actions and words earn him the title of Arch-anti-Semite. Not only did Boyle defend the PLO, but he also actively worked to advance its genocidal goals.

I do not mean to call every supporter of the idea of a Palestinian state an anti-Semite. In this situation, we are speaking of the Palestine Liberation Organization, a terrorist group, and it's fair to call all Palestinian terrorist groups anti-Semitic and their supporters thus anti-Semites. We are speaking of a time period before the Oslo Accords, which is when the PLO declared itself to be two organizations: the Fateh terrorist group and the Palestinian Authority. I do not believe a simple name change automatically dissolves one of hatred, and in this case the PLO has not separated itself from its original objectives. In the case of the Palestinian Authority, they are not only signatory to the Arab boycott of Israel, but they actively propagate it. And just like joining or supporting any group that espouses hatred as part of its platform, supporting the Palestinian Authority is supporting of the anti-Semitic Arab boycott of Israel; thus, the PA supporters are anti-Semitic.

Further proving Professor Boyle wants to destroy Israel, in the same article he proposes a peace plan in which he outlines several steps, the first of which is to "immediately move for the *de facto* suspension of Israel throughout the entirety of the United Nations system, including the General Assembly and all U.N. subsidiary organs and bodies." In doing this, Professor Boyle is stating he wants to delegitimize Israel as a nation. If this were to pass, Arab attacks on Israel would not be considered acts of war. This suspension would inherently allow any government in the world to claim the land of Israel as theirs. Israel would thus cease to exist on the international stage, if Boyle gets his way.

In his "peace" plan, Professor Boyle also states, "We must move to have the U.N. General Assembly adopt comprehensive economic, diplomatic, and travel sanctions against Israel..." Boyle is proposing to deny all economic cooperation and trade with Israel, plus forbidding anyone the ability to enter or leave Israel, thus converting all of Israel into another Warsaw Ghetto. Boyle's plan would facilitate his first objective of having all Arab nations attack Israel, since his Warsaw Ghetto plan would effectively starve out all of Israel and not just economically, which is expressly mentioned in this point of his plan. Boyle's plan is to roundup and lockup Jews into one central area where they cannot escape or get any help, while a delegitimized people are left defense-less. This sounds oddly familiar.

Furthermore, Professor Boyle wants Israel to be held accountable for genocide and war crimes against the Palestinians, which have never occurred. To top it off, Boyle stated that, "Concerned citizens and governments all over the world must organize a comprehensive campaign of economic disinvest-ment and divestment from Israel," which is the furthering of the Arab boycott. Since this declaration was made as part of his official capacity as the legal rep-resentative of the Palestine Liberation Organization, that makes the expanded boycott call, the campaign of "disinvestment and divestment from Israel," an illegal foreign boycott as defined by U.S. Antiboycott laws. Professor Boyle, by his own words, was working for the Palestinian Authority as far back as 1987, and he officially had carte blanch to establish policy within his capac-ity as legal advisor to the Palestine Liberation Organization negotiating team. This campaign for "disinvestment and divestment from Israel" was created within his official capacity with the PLO. Boyle, however, did not stop there.

In May of 2002, Boyle also had an article published in Counterpunch mag-azine[9], which is self-defined as "muckraking with a radical attitude." In his article "In Defense of a Disinvestment Campaign Against Israel," Boyle starts by discussing his work in "drafting of the Palestinian Declaration Indepen-dence." Despite completing that document, that declaration was never issued, once again proving my point about the Palestinians not being able to declare a state for political-religious reasons. This declaration was, however, meant to be more of a public relations stunt than an actual meaningful declaration. As Boyle stated when discussing the wording, he "purposefully sought to commu-nicate with Americans in terms the Palestinians thought the Americans could readily comprehend and sympathize with." According to Boyle, the Palestin-ian Declaration of Independence is more about sympathy than an actual state, thus leading me to believe Boyle fully knows and agrees with the plan of a Pal-estinian state in place of, and not alongside, Israel. Boyle wrote the Palestinian Declaration of Independence as part of his official duties is a public relations tool, nothing else.

---

9. www.counterpunch.org

This was not the first public relations campaign by the Palestinians. I have heard reports going back as far as the 1970s or 1980s of the terrorist Palestine Liberation Organization hiring a major New York public relations firm, but it is difficult to make the murderers of women and children look good, especially as they openly continue to pursue their murderous terrorist campaigns. That may be how the Palestine Liberation Organization came up with the politically correct term "armed struggle" to redefine their terrorism, so that Americans would sympathize with them. Boyle inherently wants Americans, well, probably not American Jews, to sympathize with terrorists and terrorist supporters in order to facilitate the creation of a Palestinian state instead of saying terrorist murder is wrong. The words "armed struggle" became part of the very boycott campaign Boyle initiated.

Boyle states that he gave campus lectures in the fall of 2000 which called for "the establishment of a nationwide campaign of divestment/disinvestment against Israel," the campaign he originally conceived when working as a high level consultant to the PLO. In the same article, Boyle further states his goal is to "dismantle its criminal apartheid regime against the Palestinian People living in occupied Palestine as well as in Israel itself." The claim about Israel using apartheid methods has already been refuted here. Boyle just uses the apartheid claim as a false justification for his call of "dismantling… Israel itself." Boyle's goal is to dismantle Israel, rather than solve the alleged apartheid he can't prove exists, because it in fact does not exist.

In the case of South African and actual apartheid, the goal was to abolish the law and bring the majority black population into the government. That is not the goal of Boyle and his appalling campaign. The Palestinians and their supporters wish to destroy the entire majority government of Israel and remove the population, replacing it with minority Palestinian Arab population rule. The goals of the two campaigns, therefore, are in diametrical opposition, proving again that Boyle is only interested in destroying Israel.

Most importantly, Boyle reaffirmed that he conceived and created the divestment-from-Israel campaign when working as a consultant for the PLO, which was signatory to the Arab boycott of Israel long before becoming the Palestine Authority. On the topic of Boyle working for the Palestine Liberation Organization and the Palestinian Authority, I may not be a lawyer, but I have wondered if Boyle, in his capacity as a negotiator for a foreign entity, had to register with the U.S. Department of Justice as a foreign agent in compliance with the Foreign Agents Registration Act (FARA). There are no records of his registration. In fact, considering the amount of direct activity Boyle had with the Palestine Liberation Organization, the official name of the Palestinian delegation, I am surprised I could not locate his name in the FARA activities postings of the PLO, which are located on the FARA website. CAIR, the Council on American-Islamic Relations, an organization where news commentator Debbie Schlussel was one of the first people to reveal its terrorist associations, is listed in the PLO's FARA filings as meeting with the PLO's delegation.

Most revealing of its true intentions is the official logo of the Palestine Liberation Organization to the United States. The logo is not limited to parts of Israel or any occupied territories. The official PLO map of the proposed Palestine, as evidenced by its official logo on all official correspondences, is a map of the entire state of Israel being the state of Palestine. That logo is still official today and if I were the Prime Minister of Israel, I would never negotiate with any entity that officially stated the desire to steal my entire nation; however, the United States government continues to demand Israel negotiate with the PLO despite the logo demonstrating its true intent. Israel is and has been arm-twisted into negotiating with the PLO, a terrorist entity sworn to Israel's destruction, which in turn refuses to negotiate in good faith.

The divest-from-Israel campaign changed the landscape of the three-phase plan by becoming Phase Two, since the interim state concept was for all practical purposes nullified by the acceptance of a final status leaving Israel in existence, which contradicts the objectives of the entire Arab League, Palestine Liberation Organization and Palestinian Authority. The pressing global boycott and economic isolation of Israel became central to the plan to destroy Israel. If Phase Two, the economic devastation of Israel, becomes a reality, then Phase Three kicks in: dismantlement. Boyle's plan to isolate Israel and lock all Jews in a delegitimized Israel as his new Warsaw Ghetto idea would be fulfilled in that stage. Therefore, Boyle presented an approach to fully enact Phase Two of the Palestine Liberation Organization plan to facilitate Israel's destruction by legal maneuverings instead of brute force.

The Arabs are looking forward to the day their economic isolation plans are fulfilled so they can claim Israel is not viable and should be dismantled rather than bailed out. This is the new three-phase plan to destroy Israel: it must be stopped. When you hear boycott, divestment, disinvestment or other economic campaigns against Israel, you now know these plans are all designed to separate people, rather than bring people together for peace. Plans such as these do nothing but isolate Israel and eventually bring about its destruction. Peace is neither part of Boyle's plan nor can it be achieved by following his divest-from-Israel plan or any other plans, all of which are part of the Palestine Liberation Organization/Palestinian Authority goal to destroy Israel.

Furthering the Arab Boycott

any businesses have purposely, and some unwittingly, furthered the Arab boycott of Israel. People need to be aware of such cases in order to avoid involving themselves in spreading this illegal and anti-Semitic action. Requests for compliance or even mere inquires for information that further the boycott can trigger legal dilemmas; therefore, it is best for businesses to avoid any involvement.

I have personally been involved with the following important cases, all of which have had far reaching implications regarding Middle East peace. All contributions to the boycott further the separation of people and thus thwart peace, not enhance it. These cases demonstrate how the boycott blocks and destroys peace, as well as the stealthy ways that foreign government policies have affected American businesses and perhaps, even you.

eBay

When I encounter businesses that blatantly violate U.S. Antiboycott laws, I do not start by making accusations. My primary goal in these situations is to educate the company, because I refuse to fault people for inadvertent errors. When a business wants to correct a mistake, I am more than happy to work with them. On the other hand, if I discover I am dealing with purposeful attacks on Israel, I will have no mercy, because I have little tolerance for people who make excuses to justify their hate. Oddly enough, I have more respect for blatant hate-mongers than excuse makers because at least they admit their hate and I know where they stand.

Major corporations are usually straightforward with their guidelines and generally have strict policies against discriminatory tactics, including requests for refusal to conduct business with Israel. When I run into problems communicating with major companies, it is usually because I have come in contact with public relations people who are more worried about keeping their own jobs and making others happy than actually solving problems. Many PR people see themselves as virtual corporate psychologists; they act like slick salespeople telling the public to be happy with company policies and that everything in the world is wonderful due to such practices. This is especially true when public relations work is outsourced; these PR people do not have a direct stake in the firms they represent. In my experience, PR people love to claim they know how to respond to boycotts, even when lacking experience or professional knowledge. I specialize in political and consumer boycotts, especially the Arab boycott. Boycotts are a specialty. My specialty. I have met with several public relations disasters dealing with boycotts and have found that in some cases, PR people do not understand that putting frosting on a cake is not always the correct answer. In those cases, I find myself climbing the corporate ladder to find the right people to resolve problems, not because I want to, but because it must be done. Such is the case when I encountered eBay.

On Wednesday, September 30, 2009, I received an email from a Boycott Watch reader in New York State informing me about an eBay auction with the following wording in its terms and conditions of sale: "Worldwide shipping except Israel." This immediately set off red flags for illegal compliance regarding the Arab boycott. My investigation showed the seller in question had that stipulation in every auction posted. This particular seller was in Malaysia, the very country where Yasser Arafat was promoting the Arab boycott, while ironically negotiating a peace treaty with Israeli Prime Minister Ehud Barak and President Clinton. The Malaysia factor raised even more alarm flags for being a primary nation boycotting Israel. The population of Malaysia is more than 60% Muslim: Sultan Mizan Zainal Abidin is the primarily ceremonial king; Mohamed Najib bin Abdul Razak is the Prime Minister; and Muhyiddin bin Mohamed Yassin is the Deputy Prime Minister. The country's leaders are clearly Muslim, which certainly explains why Arafat helped expand the Arab boycott there. Although Malaysia is not an Arab country per se, the Islamic kinship made Malaysia a prime expansion target for the Palestinian Authority.

Upon further investigation, I discovered over 1600 such auctions on eBay, which explicitly denied sales and shipment to Israel. Not all of those auctions took place in Malaysia, and I had no way of determining how long eBay was allowing such auctions to exist. I had a difficult time finding contact information for eBay to address the problem, but eventually discovered its media contact phone number, which I called and left a message. In my reporting capacity with Boycott Watch, I regularly call the media phone numbers of businesses. Callbacks are not uncommon with media lines, because many businesses first make sure they are speaking to actual media before commenting. As is also common, I received a callback by someone wanting to gather information such as my deadline before issuing a statement. Since this report is not about the PR firm, I will leave those names out and only refer the individual as PR Agent X.

It turned out a major public relations firm, which eBay had contracted, employed PR Agent X. As I expected, PR Agent X had no idea what I was talking about at first. Though I discussed the Arab boycott and relevant legal issues, the agent essentially did nothing. Despite PR Agent X promising to get me a response from eBay by the close of the business day Monday night, I ended up having to make countless phone calls only to be told that PR Agent X was in a meeting thus apparently had no real intention of responding. That placed me on the verge of posting a report to the Boycott Watch website and then sending it to the major media outlets. My report would have stated eBay was indifferent to discrimination against Israel. Personally, I do not understand why a discrimination issue was not treated as a high priority. When I finally spoke to PR Agent X Monday night almost a week later, it became abundantly clear she was wasting my time since she had taken no action at all. As a result, I had to tell PR Agent X in very firm words that I needed to speak to someone at eBay itself immediately because I didn't not want to chastise eBay for her inactions. As a member of the media, I expect to receive answers to my legitimate questions as promised, and rightfully so. Silence means indifference, and in this case I believe the indifference came from PR agent X and not directly from eBay, hence my demands to speak to someone from eBay directly.

Although it was after 5PM in California time, I finally got to speak with an eBay representative within thirty minutes. This person understood the urgency of the issue, as one could vicariously interpret the silence of PR Agent X to mean that eBay was complicit about violating discrimination laws. In my call, I explained the law to Evonne Gomez, Senior Public Relations Specialist at eBay, and went over the relevant sections of the law, which can be found with other applicable discrimination laws on the United States Department of Commerce website. I also explained eBay had in all likelihood inadvertently allowed illegal auction stipulations to exist, but eBay was probably not aware of the specific auction stipulations, did not know the law, and was therefore not proactively taking precautionary measures. I could have just turned the case information over to the Department of Commerce for full investigation, but I would rather give people the benefit of the doubt. My goal is not to punish people for honest mistakes; rather, the important questions were how eBay would react and how long would it take to rectify the problem. While eBay's PR representative wanted a few days to research the issue, I was tired of all the delays, I said, "I am not playing games here" and informed Ms. Gomez that I expected an immediate response. This was a clear case of discrimination and illegal foreign boycott because the sale and shipping stipulations specifically excluded national affiliation and destination. To its credit, eBay issued the following statement in less than one business day:

> The eBay User Agreement requires all users to comply with applicable law. Under U.S. law, listings that offer 'worldwide shipping excluding Israel' are not permitted and will be removed from eBay.

In part, I sent the following reply to eBay:

> Congratulations on complying with the law. At last check there were 1,611 auctions with the words 'excluding Israel' in the auction body, and I see searching for auctions with those words now have zero results. In the meantime, auction 'Thomas The Tank Engine Coloring Book & 110's Stickers' is still active and contains the following:
>
> Shipping & Handling: We ship WORLDWIDE except Israel.'
>
> Additionally, the seller of that item, 'littlewf'[1] who refused to ship to Israel with any and all of that sellers auctions are still active and so are all of that sellers auctions. Please let me know when eBay expects to be in full compliance with U.S. Antiboycott laws. Please also inform your legal department that they may want to disclose the situation and the fact they rectified it to the BIS[2], as well as filing IRS form 5713—'International Boycott Report' for all years eBay has been in violation of said laws.

Within minutes of sending that email, I received a reply from Ms. Gomez informing me those auctions were removed, which I confirmed when refreshing the page. To their credit, Ms. Gomez and eBay took the appropriate action when confronted with the fact that people were using eBay to practice

1.active on eBay since November of 2003
2.the Bureau of Industry and Security under the United States Department of Commerce

discrimination against Israel in violation of U.S. Antiboycott statutes and other applicable laws.

This case serves as an important lesson about the imperative of not being silent when companies comply with illegal and discriminatory foreign boycott practices. I am certain that many eBay sellers will attempt to circumvent eBay's new policy. It's human nature. I realize eBay is strict in its monitoring for policy violations, but that does not mean it will be or even can be expected to be perfect. As I always tell people, if they see something questionable, please contact me via the Boycott Watch website, www.BoycottWatch.com. I read all emails and do my best to reply to every one. As demonstrated with this situation, I investigate cases myself and then take action.

The eBay case may not be over. While auctions by sellers like "littlewf" were removed, some have reappeared on eBay without restrictive stipulations in their actions. This does not, however, mean the sellers will ship their goods to Israel. Nor does it mean all businesses will comply with U.S. Antiboycott laws. If you come across a similar situation, remember that you are not just dealing with a case of a single product unable to reach you. You may very likely be dealing with a situation of anti-Semitism and individuals who want to further the Arab-Israel conflict. In those cases, the person may very likely enjoy battling you rather than shipping your paid item or other desired items to you in Israel. If the person or company you bought the item from has a U.S. connection, please consider reporting that sale to the U.S. Department of Commerce, Office of Antiboycott Compliance. The law states that "no U.S. persons" shall engage in a foreign boycott of nations friendly to the United States, and the term "U.S. persons" means anyone within the U.S., its territories and companies with a U.S. presence. The company eBay, as an intermediary sales agent, is covered under this law even if the buyer and seller are not in the United Stated. The law is far reaching and is there for good reason: to prevent foreign entities from creating *de facto* U.S. foreign trade policy. The law is in place so let's use it.

Dubai Ports World

P&O Ports was a privately held British shipping port management firm that owned and operated many shipping ports globally. In 2005, a business deal was being developed to sell that company, including the management of American ports, to Dubai Ports World, a company fully owned by the United Arab Emirates, a nation signatory to the Arab boycott. The Bush administration had pushed the deal, claiming it was in the best interests of the United States, but the public did not see it that way. The deal was touted as completed when announced, and it almost was. Upon hearing the news, Americans were outraged that a foreign government, not just a foreign based company, would be managing U.S. ports, especially since many Americans viewed the Emirates as having connections to known terrorists due to several 9/11 hijackers coming from its neighbor, Saudi Arabia.

The Bush administration pressed the deal, publicly claiming the company managing the ports is not responsible for port security. For political reasons, the Bush administration refrained from saying the 'country' managing the ports, instead preferring to downplay the fact with the term 'company'; however, Americans rightfully interpreted those statements as being a foreign government would control our ports. That outraged the American public, which did not want to place U.S. ports in the hands of a foreign government with questionable ties.

In response to the unexpected public outrage, the Bush administration changed its rhetoric to claim the job of port security is the responsibility of the Department of Homeland Security and the U.S. Coast Guard, an obvious ploy meant to pacify the outraged nation. It didn't work. Americans, especially after 9/11, take security very seriously. The reality is Americans feel an inherent security responsibility at their home, workplace, and country as a whole. Regardless of being a gun owner or against personal gun ownership, for example, Americans are much more aware of their surroundings than ever and no longer take their personal security for granted. Farming out port security to foreign governments, in particular those with tangential ties to terrorists was unthinkable for the American public, especially to President Bush's conservative base.

Americans also realized that the company managing the ports has special and privileged access to all shipments, timetables, routes, physical container content, bills of lading, secure holding areas and, most worrisome to intelligence analysts, access to information about secret U.S. shipments around the world. This would include the content, origin and destination of all internationally shipped goods. Port operators could easily offer this information to unfriendly foreign agents and nations without the U.S. government knowing it; thus, foreign management can create an intelligence security nightmare for the U.S. While the United Arab Emirates is somewhat friendly to the United States and allows United States Naval ships to dock there, there is far more to the United Arab Emirates story than just that.

The United Arab Emirates was formed in 1971 as the federation of seven Emirates, including Dubai. The U.A.E. has limited federal powers, leaving many governmental powers to the member emirates. Not all member Emirates are part of the federation court system, which has both civil and Islamic courts. The Islamic courts rule over all family matters; not surprisingly, women do not have the right to vote anywhere in the U.A.E. This raised certain questions about human rights with the possible ports deal—should our ports be operated by a nation that denies women the right to vote? Would women who work in U.S. ports managed by Dubai Ports World face overt or inherent bigotry since Dubai advocates gender discrimination? These are questions Dubai never answered, and I interpreted it as a danger sign. It is an issue American unions should have championed on behalf of its members. The misogynistic denial of the right of women to vote by the parent company could have also affected women in management, as they may have been denied promotion or corporate travel in any form.

Amongst the issues I raised was that the United Arab Emirates is a major drug transshipment point for Southwest Asian drug producing countries. Being a major financial center makes the U.A.E. ideal for money laundering, which is often associated with the drug trade. The U.A.E. has undefined and open borders with Saudi Arabia and Oman; this allows drugs and other goods, including weapons, to be moved between those countries without scrutiny. A Middle East open-borders crisis occurred in 2002 when North Korean Scud missiles were shipped to Yemen; shockingly, the scud missiles suddenly vanished. This inherently makes U.A.E. management of U.S. ports the ideal transshipment point for terrorist smugglers to ship hazardous cargo into the U.S. Considering that Yemen was the focal point of an attempted terrorist attack against the United States in 2009, the security concerns of the American public were justified since Dubai managed ports would have been the perfect terrorist access point. Blocking the 2002 Dubai Ports World deal, therefore, prevented at least one major terrorist attack against the United States in 2009.

While the U.S. would surely catch the vast majority off such dangerous shipments, potential terrorists in the United States who would receive such shipments would not be scared of U.S. domestic courts if they were willing to be suicide bombers anyhow. Let's face it. The 9-11 terrorists would rather be on trial in civilian courts in New York City than face military tribunals; therefore, just one such shipment out of thousands getting past port security and into the United States would be devastating. It would only take one dirty bomb shipment to cause a catastrophic terrorist attack, and the possibility of facing nonmilitary/domestic courts gives the enemy fewer fears to committing terrorist activities. The odds may be in our favor, but we cannot afford anything less than perfect security, so granting a possible security hole to a foreign government or even the chance for minimal punishment if caught is ludicrous.

In the context of Middle East peace, the United Arab Emirates is a member of the Arab League and a signatory member of the Arab boycott. The U.A.E. forbids Israeli products, including Israeli components in finished goods, in any Arab country. A recent U.S. Trade Representative report on trade barriers states that the U.A.E. no longer enforces the secondary and tertiary aspects of the boycott; however, the U.A.E. enforces the primary boycott and "occasional government contracts continue to contain pro forma provisions requiring a contractual obligation to 'observe all regulations and instructions enforced from time to time by the League of Arab States regarding the boycott of Israel especially those related to blacklisted companies, ships, and persons.'" In other words, the U.A.E. does not enforce a secondary boycott of Israel unless they say so. And in general, they say so. This is because the United Arab Emirates must attract American business, especially now with the economic difficulties in Dubai; thus, the U.A.E. will enforce the Arab boycott at all levels as long as they can get away with it while still trading with American companies. The U.A.E. is neither friendly to Israel nor does it want any Israeli products in their member Emirates.

In shipping, a "bill of lading" is documentation accompanying every shipment by truck, train, ship and virtually every business-to-business commercial package. It is sometimes seen as the plastic envelope on the side of packages. The bill of lading documents the shipping origin, destination, contents, quantities and price. It is essentially a detailed invoice for the goods shipped; in the case of international shipping, multiple copies may be required for customs officials. Should the Dubai Ports deal had come to fruition, the U.A.E. would have been able to examine detailed information about all shipments to and from Israel, a nation the U.A.E. actively boycotts. Even if such information is guaranteed to remain in the U.S., digital copies of such data can still easily be made and emailed globally. The Dubai Ports World deal would supply the Arab world with information about all items shipped from Israel to the United States. Armed with that information, Arab nations would be able to offer alternative products to U.S. buyers, thereby creating a trade barrier for Israeli exporters. In fact, by Dubai having such information, the Arab world would have been able to launch a full-scale economic war against Israel by using shipping information to enact total disruption of Israeli exports to the U.S. and around the world. Additionally, this information could further the Arab boycott in the United States, as the Arab countries could use knowledge of which companies were either buying or selling goods to Israeli businesses. This would have facilitated the mass expansion of the boycott far beyond what Boyle and Palestine Liberation Organization/Palestinian Authority could have ever dreamed.

This is not a cloak and dagger fantasy, as having Dubai Ports World managed ports would have also made shipping military goods to Israel difficult. Tanks, trucks and other large military hardware do not fit into shipping containers; thus, they cannot be easily hidden. Even U.S. arms shipments to Israel would have to be labeled and detailed to ensure proper and safe handling of military ordinance for safety reasons. Information about those shipments would have been automatically handed over to the government of Dubai and the United Arab Emirates—and thus the entire Arab League. The United States uses commercial shipping and therefore would have been telling every Arab nation exactly what U.S. military goods Israel has received. This is not information the U.S. or Israel wants in the hands of countries sworn to Israel's destruction, as it would telegraph Israel's military capabilities and weaknesses to the entire Arab world.

The Dubai Ports World deal would have been a much larger threat to Israel than Iran, for several reasons. First, every Arab nation would know the secrets of Israel's military and industrial capabilities. Second, war with Iran would be a single distant front and not have the multiple land-based warfronts an all out Arab attack on Israel would present. Third, knowing Israel's exact capabilities and weaknesses, partially derived from knowing what has been shipped, would allow Arabs advance planning to counter Israel via specific weaknesses, possibly even dividing the Israeli military command in the event of a conflict. Fourth, even if Iran manages to develop a nuclear device, it would likely be too fragile to survive a rocket launch. Iran would need several years to beef up that technology and in the meantime, they do not have a device they can supply for immediate strategic terrorist attacks. Information from the Dubai Ports World deal would have provided the Arab world enough immediate information to destroy Israel relatively quickly and without, pardon the pun, any fallout.

This is why just the supply of information alone is a vital element of U.S. Antiboycott laws. Information is imperative in intelligence work and can be used against nations. This is also why the divest-from-Israel advocates specifically target Caterpillar Corporation, an American business that makes heavy equipment essential for building the infrastructure needed to sustain and build nations. A boycott by Caterpillar and spare parts manufacturers alone would mean Israel would be unable to maintain itself as a nation within a few short years. Imagine the results of creating a globally coordinated boycott of Israel based on first hand knowledge of Israel's economic footing. After the information exchange, permanent damage would be done without the ability to rectify the problem.

Americans spoke out and rejected President Bush's plan to effectively hand over U.S. ports, due to fears of granting such powers to a foreign Arab nation, but that was not seen as a valid objection in today's age of political correctness. This situation is close to me personally, for it was my work that helped bring down the Dubai Ports World deal. I dug up and reminded the world about the long forgotten and unglamorous U.S. Antiboycott laws. I had reminded the world about the Arab boycott pertaining to this case in an article published on the Boycott Watch website and IsraelNationalNews.com, to name a few. Several other publications picked up this article, and they pointed out how dangerous it would be to Israel should Dubai Ports World run U.S. ports. My article and points were used almost verbatim by groups like the Anti-Defamation League and the American Israel Public Affairs Committee (AIPAC), without giving me credit for my work. While I would have liked to receive proper credit, no writer had published any articles about how the Dubai Ports World deal related to the Arab boycott prior to mine. Without mentioning specific names, some major writers whom I know follow my work picked up my ideas and ran with them as their own.

The public outrage created by my work was intense. The Arab boycott of Israel and the potential harm of the Dubai Ports World deal reached Congress and the media. Within days of the Arab boycott becoming the single focal point of the deal's opponents, President Bush backed off. The Arab boycott was the single key issue that took down the deal, much to the chagrin of President Bush. In the end, America and freedom were the domestic winners, and Israel was potentially saved.

Beyond Boycotts

CHAPTER 8

s we know, the Arab boycott was origi-
nally formed to starve out the Jews and
prevent Israel from being established.
After Israel's inception, however, the Arab boycott
campaign had to adjust to contend with potential
cross-border trade between Israel and Arab nations,
rather than simply the local and regional trade relations within what became Israel's borders. The
global expansion of the boycott needed plausible
justification because simply boycotting for the
sake of boycotting does not work, and the Arabs
knew this. They did not recognize Israel's right to

exist anyhow, so the target of the boycott was, by their definition, against the Zionists. Despite acknowledging that not all Zionists lived in Israel, the Arabs viewed all Zionists, and all Jews for that matter, as fair game. The boycott plan therefore shifted to the financial devastation of all Jews worldwide regardless of any actual Israeli association. The Arabs recognized all Jews as Zionists—that was all they needed to know.

To sell the boycott globally, the Arabs created the campaign of "Zionism Equals Racism," which had a simple message. By claiming all Zionists were bad, the Arabs felt their global boycott response was justified. Of course, this completely fabricated claim is equally disproved by the same basic facts that discredit the apartheid claim, yet they repeated the lie in hopes it would catch on as fact without proof. To some it did. Just like the apartheid claim, the racism assertion was strictly meant to distract the public; the idea was to have the public blindly accept the racism charge, thereby shifting the argument to Zionism is racism. It is the classic bait and switch tactic applied to Israel and its right to exist. The concept of "Zionism Equals Racism" took a long time to be accepted; amazingly the United Nations even adopted it on November 10, 1975, in Resolution 3379: "Zionism is a form of racism and racial discrimination." In the meantime, fabricated books such as the *Protocols of the Elders of Zion*, were being spread around and promoted as Jewish conspiracies to take over the world.

When the Arab boycott began taking a more stealth approach in the United States due to U.S. Antiboycott laws, it was still being pressed in the rest of the world. The boycott presently flourishes in nations such as France, with its growing Muslim population, and in England where the academic boycott of Israel is prevalent. These European governments literally deny the writings and ideas from Israeli scholars. The academic boycotts are the witch hunt for Jewish thought and book burnings on a both virtual and real level. It is all part of the greater plan to isolate Israel from the rest of the world, and these efforts will eventually intensify over time.

With the advent of the Oslo Accords, a new paradigm was needed to deal with the Palestinian agreement to accept a Palestinian state with Israel existing, which again contrasts previously stated Palestinian goals. The Arab street inherently rejected the Oslo Accords' changes to their long standing goals of the complete destruction of Israel. The Palestinian rejection of Oslo, a plan for two states living side-by-side in peace, can be seen at the website of the Middle East Media and Research Institute: www.memri.org. MEMRI, as it is more commonly known, posts highlights of the Arab media, such as interviews of both national and religious leaders openly calling for the complete destruction of Israel. This rhetoric includes videos where Yasser Arafat openly calls for peace in English one day, yet the next day screams "Jihad, Jihad, Jihad" to his Palestinian constituents the next. Despite what Palestinian Authority leaders may say to the rest of the world, the norm in the Arab media, including on Al-Jazeera Television which has an office and broadcast studio in Washington, D.C., is to call for Israel's complete annihilation.

Despite the constant attacks of Israel on Al-Jazeera, one opposing view was accidentally aired live on Al-Jazeera Television Qatar on February 21, 2006, because Al-Jazeera did not know what the guest would say. Thanks to MEMRI, a video of Arab-American psychiatrist Dr. Wafa Sultan can be seen on their website with English subtitles where she harshly criticizes the Arab world for being "backwards" and living in the past. The show's misogynist host was clearly shocked by what he was hearing and didn't believe the ideas came from a woman. In that broadcast, Dr. Sultan criticized the Islamic world for treating "women like beasts." Dr. Sultan went on to criticize how Islam chastises non-Muslims and then said to let Jews and Christians "have their beliefs." Not surprisingly, she was called a heretic for her honesty.

In her criticism, Dr. Sultan spoke about the accomplishments of Jews that should be respected and remarked how Jews do not commit suicide bombings in restaurants, destroy churches, destroy religious symbols such as the three Buddha statues, or burn down embassies the way Muslims do in the name of Islam. According to Dr. Sultan, destructive paths, which inherently include boycotts, are the antithesis of peace building.

I drove to Detroit, Michigan one day to hear Nonie Darwish speak. Ms. Darwish is the daughter of an Egyptian army general and the author of *Now They Call Me Infidel; Why I Renounced Jihad for America, Israel and the War on Terror.* In her wonderful lecture, Ms. Darwish did not address the Arab boycott. I asked if she felt that the boycott were an issue to which she immediately agreed and then went into great detail with her perspective of the issue, essentially agreeing with me. Later that evening, I accidentally met Ms. Darwish and her delegation while having dinner at the same restaurant. The company and conversation that evening was wonderful, and I gained some valuable insight into the ingrained nature of the Arab hatred toward all Jews, and not just Israelis. Ms. Darwish explained how from the time she was a child, Jews have always been chastised; sadly, this is normal in the Arab world. This ingrained hatred is passed on from generation to generation, and what is also sad is how the American media accepts such hatred within Arab society. While our media harshly attacks gay-bashing and anti African-American bigotry, Arab anti-Semitism is not treated in the same light; rather, many often chastise Israel with the fake apartheid claim.

In response to Yasser Arafat openly calling for peace in English one day and screaming "Jihad, Jihad, Jihad" the next, I have heard media pundits claim Arafat was just placating his constituents: that is an absurd claim. Arafat never had to face voters since the Palestinian Authority did not have real elections. By their own internal policy, Palestinians will not agree to a Palestinian state consisting of anything less than all of Israel. For the Palestinians, anything less than a full state would be unacceptable since a complete Palestine in place of Israel has always been their single objective. Accepting anything less by Arafat or his successors is unacceptable, unless the Arab street is sold on the idea of the "interim Palestinian state," which is part of the three-phase plan discussed in Chapter 6. Despite this, Yasser Arafat had created and promised an all-or-nothing vision of Palestine, and the people will now not settle for anything less. Failure to deliver anything less than what was promised may result in a Palestinian civil war. The Oslo Accords do seem to have thus resulted in the Palestinians creating an untenable situation for themselves.

In his aforementioned 2002 article "Law and Disorder in the Middle East," Francis Anthony Boyle spells out his campaign to vilify Israel. The arguments he uses are the same ones heard in the media against Israel and include silly claims that Israel is committing war crimes against Palestinians daily. Let's examine those claims along with Boyle's charges. One does not have to be a lawyer to see the gaping holes in his assertions.

First, Boyle states that today's problems started when Prime Minister Ariel Sharon stepped foot on the Temple Mount in Jerusalem, what the Arabs call the Al-Haram al-Sharif. While that site is considered the third holiest site in Islam, it is actually the single holiest site in Judaism, for that is where the Beit Hamigdash, the Holy Temple of the Bible, stood. Boyle, along with Palestinians, like to claim the years of Arab riots that occurred right after that event are the sole result of Sharon's actions, but they fail to mention that this violence followed a short lull in hostilities between Arabs and Jews at the time. They also fail to mention that Ariel Sharon only became Prime Minister in 2001, long after their campaign began. The Arab world used Sharon as an excuse to justify violence and terrorism as if nothing ever preceded that day, and the general media bought it. The world seemed to blame Israel for the terrorist actions of Palestinian thugs as though the Palestinians had zero responsibility for their own actions. There may have been a lull, but the two sides were still at war all the same.

What Boyle fails to mention in his article is that the riots that began after Prime Minister Sharon took just a few steps onto the Temple Mount not only demonstrated the intolerance of Islam to other religions, but also where apartheid really exists. Israel allows people of all faiths to pray at the Western Wall, which is located just below the Temple Mount, without checking religious pedigree. Muslims, however, forbid all non-Muslims and especially Jews from being anywhere near their mosque. That is hardly a sign of religious tolerance or acceptance. Furthermore, the fact that riots would be blamed on a single incident indicates the disdain Muslims have toward Jews and Judaism in particular. Reaching far beyond Jerusalem, there is no Islamic tolerance of Jews in the Middle East. One can only drive to Hebron, for example, in bulletproof and caged busses due to the constant attacks on Jews driving on the dedicated Jewish road to Hebron that leads to their homes. I have ridden on those busses and can tell you first hand that it was dangerous. I have personally witnessed the plethora of Muslim men, women and children who have zero tolerance for Jews living or visiting there, attacking us repeatedly. Just another lovely day in Hebron.

As for the alleged war crimes, Boyle makes a simple assertion: "We all have a general idea of what a war crime is, so I will not elaborate upon the term." That was Boyle's way of making a claim without having to explain its basis, which he can't. Boyle is making the slanted proverbial, "Do you still beat up your wife" charge, which is meant to assert guilt without the basis of proof. He has also made specific claims that are ludicrous and erroneous to the point of defamation:

> Since the start of the Al Aqsa Intifada[1], the world has seen those heinous war crimes inflicted every day by Israel against the Palestinians in occupied Palestine: e.g., willful killing of Palestinian civilians by the Israeli army and by Israel's illegal paramilitary settlers.

Let's examine that charge in detail.

First, Boyle believes Israel is violating the Fourth Geneva Convention, which refers to an occupying power, because Israel is not responding to Palestinian terrorism symmetrically. The main problem with this claim is that since signing the Oslo Accords, there is no occupation—the Palestinians have complete autonomy including police powers; in fact, Israel even supplies them with weapons. There is no such thing as "autonomous occupation"—it is an oxymoron. Second, since there was never any state which extended civil law over Gaza, that land cannot be considered as ever being owned by a "High Contracting Party," the legal definition of a state in international law. Only land which is part of another nation which comes under the military control of another nation can be considered occupied. Third, when Jordan gave up its claim to Judea and Samaria, that land became stateless; therefore it too, cannot be considered as occupied. As a professor of international law, Boyle must know he is making a public relations claim and not a legitimate legal claim.

The only reason there is no declared state of Palestine is that the Palestinians have not declared one; otherwise, they would have to begin taking full responsibility for their own state and finally appreciate that Israel is an autonomous, separate country. The Palestinians had Boyle write a declaration of independence, and Israel is not in the position to prevent such a declaration from being read. As previously stated, the Palestinians do not want to commit to a final status under Oslo or else they will have to start living their own lives and begin accepting the reality of their situation. Even still, Israel facilitates

---

1. September 28, 2000

the Palestinian autonomous structure by supplying water, electricity and even revenue from the Israeli national tax. Israel also facilitates Palestinian trade commerce with its ports. The Palestinians have a *de facto* state and are clearly using their unofficial nation status as a tool to use Israel as a political punching bag. Beating up Israel in the media works in favor of the Palestinians, so they see no reason to change what they are doing.

Let us look at post-World War II Japan and Germany. Both countries are presently world powers with thriving economies. I do not remember Japan and Germany refusing to run their own nations and instead blaming America for their country's woes; rather, they rebuilt their nations and reputations up, and are now among the finest and wealthiest countries globally. The Palestinians do not look at those nations as models for their own future, but instead they have choose the path of perpetual hate and then claim terrorism is a justified response.

Another one of Boyle's charges that became official Palestinian Authority policy is the following: "Israeli settlers living illegally in occupied Palestine constitute war crimes." This is a blatantly false claim. By international agreement, the Palestinians govern their own area autonomously, and the Israeli Army does not enter those areas unless the situation calls for it. One such example took place during the 2006 conflict where Israel took military action to protect Israelis from rocket attacks from Gaza. In an effort to protract their battle to destroy Israel, Palestinians like to give people the impression that the occupation claim only refers to the West Bank/Judea and Samaria, which the Palestinian Authority agreed as part of the Oslo Accords. As written in that agreement, Palestinians will live in certain areas, Jews will live in certain areas, there will be some 'no man's land' as a buffer, and in some cases there will be shared areas, such as roads. With the Oslo Agreement, the Palestinians have their own specific and defined land that they administer; thus, the Palestinians negated all claims to other land.

If you look at the Palestinian Authority's official map of Palestine, you will see they consider all of what is Israel to be their Palestinian state; thus, the Palestinians consider all of Israel as occupied, which is the real basis for their occupation claim. The Palestinians own official map telegraphs the message that they will never be satisfied until they get every inch of Israel as prescribed in their original constitution. This is still stated in the constitutions of every Palestinian Authority subsidiary, including the terrorist Hamas organization that runs Gaza, which, as we may recall, was given to the Palestinians without any concessions. To the Palestinians, Israel's very existence is an occupation and war crime since they consider every inch of the land to be "occupied Palestine." This is why Israel insists on Palestinian recognition of Israel as a precondition to peace—without the complete Palestinian recognition of Israel and respect for Israeli borders, Israel would be under the continual and open threat of annihilation by the Palestinians. For that matter, recognition of Israel and its right to exist by all Arab nations is also vital for peace. While Iran is a Persian and not Arab nation, it is an example of a country that refuses to recognize Israel's right to exist and that is actively and openly seeking Israel's destruction.

Palestinians also like to claim that Israel's military response to terrorism is itself a war crime, since it is not a "symmetrical" response and because civilians are killed in the process. This is a particularly interesting claim. As demonstrated by their murderous terrorism, Palestinians view all Israelis, or Zionists as they prefer to say, because Palestinians do not recognize Israel's right to exist, as combatants and therefore legitimate targets for terrorism. That is the Palestinian justification for the murder of women, children and the elderly. Palestinians view themselves, on the other hand, as entirely civilian. By demanding a symmetrical response, Palestinians are saying they want Israel to launch random and indiscriminate attacks on Palestinian civilians which they know Israel will never do. The symmetrical response charge is therefore nothing more than a diversion from the truth.

While I was on Al-Jazeera Television, Noura Erakat complained about Israel's response to terrorism attacks in Gaza. I responded, "Where were you when S'derot was being bombed?" Noura was silent, so I kept asking that question to no avail. If she really wanted peace, she would at least have complained or acknowledged the existence of Palestinian attacks on Israeli's. Her silence proved she had no discernible objections to Palestinian attacks on Jews. Neither Israel nor any nation should sit back silently, as rockets are indiscriminately fired into cities to murder civilians. Noura, however, illustrated the unfortunate and ignorant position that the world should remain silent when Palestinians murder Israelis, yet be outraged when Jews take necessary defensive actions.

In addressing Israel's response level, military analysts will tell you Palestinian rockets have no guidance systems and are fired to murder indiscriminately. Additionally, they are meant to evoke fear since nobody ever knows where the rockets will land, how much damage the rockets will cause, or if anyone will be killed. The Israeli response to terrorism always exhibits extreme restraint. Israel takes repeated hits and only responds when there is no alternative. Israel respects the lives of others, even their enemies.

If Israel would ever retaliate with a truly symmetrical response, then it would have to respond with an equally indiscriminate attack, which is unacceptable. Instead, Israel makes precise attacks on specific terrorist leaders in order to avoid killing innocent people. The Palestinians know this, which is why terrorist leaders like to surround themselves with children as their life insurance policies or human shields. This is also why Palestinian terrorists prefer to launch their attacks on top of apartment buildings, schools, hospitals and mosques. It also explains why Israeli response attacks are rare. Israel avoids killing innocent people, whereas the Palestinians target innocent people.

A shockingly simple, yet unsigned cartoon has been making its way around the Internet, which explains the situation. In the cartoon, an Israeli soldier is kneeling in front of a baby carriage while firing at a Palestinian fighter kneeling behind a baby carriage. This cartoon is very telling and true to real life. The fact is that Israeli troops defend civilians and never position their army bases in civilian areas. Palestinians, however, launch rocket attacks from the roofs of schools, hospitals and mosques; thus, retaliatory fire can potentially end up killing civilians, which feeds into their propaganda and, quite frankly, evil behavior. The Palestinians will never admit that such placement of their military installations constitutes an actual war crime since this placement specifically puts civilians at risk. Palestinians also conveniently forget to tell people that according to international humanitarian law[2], civilian deaths during an armed conflict do not in themselves constitute war crimes. What does constitute a war crime is the bombing of cities to the ground the way the Nazis bombed London every night in order to inflict maximum civilian

---

2.the Rome Statute

damage. While Palestinian terrorism specifically targets civilians—and that is considered a true war crime—the opposite occurs when Israel responds to terrorist attacks with surgical precision. Civilians may get killed in such responses, but this is not defined as a war crime and is a far different situation: Israelis are simply trying to defend themselves as opposed to purposely murdering innocent civilians. Even the most arduous supporter of Hamas or other terrorist networks can never answer the question of why shooting rockets at civilians is acceptable. He may redirect the question, but the reality is he will never be able to give a rational response.

Perhaps nothing is more disturbing than when Palestinian parents dress their infant children up as suicide bombers and televise these images. There is no justification for such an act, and I will not even dignify this blatant child abuse with reasoning. Many such photos exist and can be found on the Internet, including pictures depicting small children learning to fire automatic rifles at Jews in combat situations. Hamas and other terrorist groups are proud to show the world photos and videos of children learning to kill Jews, lessons which ultimately raise generations to hate, thus perpetuating terrorism rather than seeking peace.

In his article, Boyle explains his war crimes argument on behalf of the Palestinian Authority, which is his campaign to justify the boycott campaign. Boyle is the architect of modern anti-Semitism. He is the ideological father of strategic planning to destroy Israel and is doing everything in his power to give Israel's enemies the capabilities to wipe the country off the map. At one point, Iranian television even reported that Boyle wanted to represent Iranian President Mahmoud Ahmadinejad, who has sworn to destroy Israel.

Boyle was also apparently unable to resist the three-phase model. His plan can be interpreted as first to create a moral equivalency between terrorism and the response to it, which in turn could debase Israel's moral standing. Second, he sought the obfuscation of the law by claiming Israel is responsible for indiscriminate targeting of civilians. Of course, this is an ironic assertion since the Palestinians, not Israelis, are the ones who fire rockets with zero guidance capability towards Israeli cities. Third, we again see the propaganda technique of Nazi Josef Goebbels: by repeating a false claim long enough, even the person who originally made up the lie will believe it. It is, in sense, a legitimized lie. That is what we are seeing—Palestinians again blaming Israel not only for the terrorism that the Palestinians initiate against Israel ironically but also for instituting apartheid. Again, however, this latter claim is completely wrong, as the Palestinians are in fact the ones promoting apartheid by restricting where Jews can live, travel and pray.

Boyle's war crimes plan may not be a boycott in itself, but it is a part of his strategic plan; therefore, it cannot be separated from the overall Arab boycott of Israel. If you really want peace with someone or some nation, you cannot achieve such harmony by making claims that facilitate its destruction, as promoted within his plan. The false war crimes claims are meant to both create the justification that anti-Semites need to openly hate Israel with impunity, and to legitimize Israel-bashing excuses.

Campuses Today

CHAPTER 9

College campuses have been the hotbed for the Arab-Israeli conflict outside of the Middle-East for decades. Prior to the Oslo Accords, and thus the creation of the Palestinian Authority, support for Palestine Liberation Organization was equated with supporting terrorism, in particular against Israeli civilians. Although it was uncommon, there were a handful of non-Arabs openly supporting the PLO, though usually as an excuse to justify their anti-Semitism. Even today, most high school students face a culture shock when first attending a university with a much more diverse population than their local high schools and having to witness or even confront PLO supporters on campuses. Colleges have always fostered free political expression, and events unfolding elsewhere inherently became a hot topic in places where students latch on to geopolitical issues.

United Nations Resolution 3379 was adopted in 1975 declaring, "Zionism is a form of racism and racial discrimination." This was not a lone anti-Israel U.N. declaration, but one that stood out of the hundreds of United Nations resolutions condemning Israel since the 1950s; the Israel bashing in the United Nations still goes on to this day. "Zionism equals Racism" had become a rallying cry by Arabs and anti-Semites in general, thereby vilifying all Jews, as evidenced by the Arab terrorism aimed at Jews globally. On campuses a new tone was set, as Jewish students suddenly came under increased fire by Arabs because the United Nations equated Jews as racists. On a global scale, it gave fuel to terrorists.

On June 27, 1976, an Air France flight originating in Tel Aviv was on its second leg of the flight from Athens to Paris, when two Germans who were assisting Palestinian terrorists from the PLO affiliate Popular Front for the Liberation of Palestine, hijacked it. After refueling, the flight was diverted to the Entebbe, Uganda airport where Uganda's dictator Idi Amin further assisted the hijackers. The flight was targeted for only one reason—there were many Jews on board since the flight originated in Israel, and Israel was the target of the hijacker's demands. The terrorists picked an Air France flight because El-Al, Israel's national airlines, was too well protected.

In a surprise raid, Israel freed the hostages in the very airport terminal that Israel had built years earlier, which is how Israel had possessed the blueprints to the structure. In the rescue, the terrorists were all killed, along with Ugandan soldiers protecting the terrorists. Sadly, Israel was not without casualties. Four of the hostages and Lieutenant Colonel Yonatan "Yoni" Netanyahu, the brother of Israeli Prime Minister Benjamin Netanyahu, also perished. Israel's daring rescue ended a long series of Arab hijackings of aircrafts, as Israel proved it would take necessary action to defend itself and not tolerate such terrorist attacks anywhere.

This event gave a moral boost to Jews worldwide. Jewish students once again became the tough guys in their schools in the short run; however, the stigma of "Zionism equals Racism" lingered. Jews still faced a public relations battle. On June 23, 1977, soon after becoming Israel's sixth Prime Minister, Menachem Begin delivered a speech in which he said, "We are all Zionists. The Land of Israel is in our hearts. Even when we were in the Dispersion, we dreamt about it, longed for it and prayed for it. This is Zion. This is the Return to Zion." The "We are all Zionists" slogan became a rallying cry by Jews worldwide, throwing the "Zionism equals Racism" resolution back in the face of the Arab world. Ironically, this line even became a popular button worn by Jews for years, to protest the United Nations resolution.

While Jews took "Zionism equals Racism" as a personal insult, the "We are all Zionists" campaign worked and the world saw the "Zionism equals Racism" resolution as the farce that it was. In fact, it became a famous joke on Saturday Night Live. In the "Weekend Update" news segment one week, anchor Chevy Chase spoke about actor Sammy Davis, Jr. converting to Judaism, attributing the punch-line "finally I can hate myself" to the black actor. The "Zionism equals Racism" resolution was only repealed because Israel made its abolition a condition for participating in the Madrid Peace Conference of 1991. Despite the repeal of that resolution, Arabs will sometimes make the absurd "Zionism equals Racism" claim on campuses as if to ask "why do you still beat your wife. Sadly, few students are versed in Israel history; thus, they remain silent when confronted with this issue.

A prime example of open anti-Semitism on campuses in the era preceding the Oslo Accords is the actress Vanessa Redgrave, who stared in a 1977 "documentary" titled "The Palestinians." In this movie, she was in a PLO training camp dancing and waving a rifle over her head. When receiving an Oscar in 1978 for the movie "Julia," Vanessa Redgrave spoke about "Zionist hoodlums" in her acceptance speech. She was, of course, speaking about all Israelis, which she reaffirmed in 1980 when she stated, "The state of Israel must be overthrown, there is no room for such a state." Putting her foot in her mouth yet again, in December 1981, the Oscar winner told the publication Arab Perspective, "The Zionist state is the cause of conflict and violence in the Middle East."

In response at the Academy Awards in 1978, screen writer Paddy Chayefsky received thunderous applauds mid-statement when he said, "I'm sick and tired of people exploiting the occasion of the Academy Awards..." After the ovation, he continued: "...for the propagation of their own personal political propaganda... a simple thank you would suffice." Statements such as those by Vanessa Redgrave, prior to the Palestine Liberation Organization being renamed the Palestinian Authority, were despicable, but for some reason today they are considered legitimate free speech. Legitimizing the concept of a Palestinian state legitimized hate speech against Jews and Israel.

Fighting terrorism was not the only issue that concerned Jewish students. In 1964, Jacob Birnbaum created The Student Struggle for Soviet Jewry (SSSJ) to win the freedom for Jews living under deplorable conditions in the Soviet Union, simply because they wanted to practice their religion. One the early leaders of SSSJ was Glenn Richter, a man who dedicated his life to the cause of freedom for Soviet Jews. The Soviet Jewry campaigns rivaled, and in many cases surpassed, the efforts by Jews fighting terrorism. It was common to see Jews in mock gulag prisons on campuses to raise awareness, which led to mass rallies including one in Washington, D.C. on Sunday, December 6, 1987, when 250,000 people gathered before a summit with President Ronald Reagan and Soviet Premier Mikhail Gorbachev.

These human rights efforts directly resulted in the struggle for religious freedoms of Christians in the Soviet Union and contributed to the ultimate demise of the entire Soviet Union. Glenn Richter worked tirelessly with students worldwide. Today the freedom of millions of people can be attributed directly to the Student Struggle for Soviet Jewry, Jacob Birnbaum, Glenn Richter and a few others. Jewish student activism worked, but the heroes remain unsung. The results of SSSJ events demonstrate the power of constructive campus activism.

The later creation of the Palestinian Authority via the Oslo Accords gave legitimacy to the pro-PLO students, as they instantly shed the pro-terrorist label and suddenly become pro-Palestine without changing one iota of their destroy-Israel philosophy. At the same time, vocal anti-Semites like Vanessa Redgrave and Yasser Arafat could pretend they were moderates by claiming they were in favor of Palestine with a new plausible denial to the attached terrorism. Anti-Semitism did not go away; instead, it just became more legitimized.

This was the new face of the Palestinians and their supporters. Criticizing people like Vanessa Redgrave suddenly became politically incorrect despite her palling around with actual terrorists with blood on their hands. The same applied to arch-terrorist Yasser Arafat—the man who planned the Munich Olympics terrorist attacks. He became an instant statesman instead of having his face on wanted posters. On campuses, the supporters of murderous terrorists also became instant "moderates."

Instead of becoming strictly political movements that would distance themselves from terrorism, the Palestinian student movements did just the opposite. The Palestinian activists and supporters did not only fail to separate themselves from pre-Oslo terrorism, but they embraced it. We see this in their ongoing attempts to conceal terrorism by claiming their actions are morally equivalent to Israel's justified responses to terrorism, and calling it the "cycle of violence." Logically, that claim means Palestinian terrorism is not only justified, but even triggered by any Israeli response to combat terrorism—that, of course, is hogwash. The Palestinian moral equivalence argument is nothing more than a way to change the topic about terrorism being evil, and passing that blame on Israel, thereby being equally bad in their eyes. They essentially argue that Israel has no right to respond to terrorism. Hate groups such as the Ku Klux Klan make the same argument, as they want to bring others down to justify their own self-inflicted miserable plight of life, rather than bringing themselves up.

The Palestinians embraced terrorism even further. The official organization which Arafat had approved to promote the divest-from-Israel campaign was the International Solidarity Movement and its American branch, the Palestinian Solidarity Movement. The ISM published a book titled *Peace Under Fire,* where I believe we can instantly visualize the group's true colors: the red blood of terrorism was seen on the jacket of the book; the color yellow could also be seen which, when combined with red, are the colors of the socialist and communist flags of oppressive nations like China. I believe the color scheme of the book was no accident, since it attracts campus Marxists and socialists. It was the ISM/PSM that somehow sneaked past Israeli tanks and enter Arafat's compound; in doing so, they lent a moral boost and aid to a besieged terrorist. The story became news headlines, instantly bringing the ISM/PSM to the forefront, especially on campuses where they primarily worked. In that private meeting, segments of which were shown on television newscasts, Arafat appeared very happy with ISM/SPM members who undoubtedly bolstered their existing pact with Arafat.

When I interviewed ISM/PSM ringleader Adam Shapiro in Columbus, Ohio at a divest-from-Israel hate festival, he said, "(the) ISM is a resource to Palestinians." He further indicated the direct relationship between his organization and the Palestinian Authority, a point later confirmed by Shapiro at the same conference, as he claimed to have established an "understanding" with Arafat that day. Shapiro also said he was banned from returning to Israel, which did not surprise me considering he blatantly disobeyed an Israeli Army order and put the lives of Israeli soldiers at risk by putting them in harm's way. I was undercover at that event and ended my rather short interview with Shapiro after following up with, "How do you feel, as a Jew, being banned from Israel?" Shapiro responded "I no longer consider myself Jewish." It was not Shapiro's self-disassociation with Judaism that ended the interview, but rather that he allowed himself to become a pawn of Middle-East politics. Despite his disavowing of Judaism, Palestinians have referred to him being Jewish in countless articles, thus giving special credence to his actions, both to justify and to recruit actual Jews to the ISM/PSM cause, including getting Jews to boycott Israel. As a leader in the ISM/PSM, Shapiro allows himself to be called Jewish when it is convenient despite his disavowing of Judaism, which is why I consider him a pawn of Middle-East politics.

The ISM/PSM showed their true affinity for terrorism when they published their book *Peace Under Fire* in 2004. On page 20 of that book in the section titled "What is the ISM?" the ISM/PSM states, "We recognize the Palestinian right to resist Israeli violence and occupation via legitimate armed struggle." In their own description of their organization, the parent group of the divest-from-Israel campaign, the ISM/PSM declared themselves as both supporters and advocates of terrorism, especially the mass terror attacks on Jews around the world, not just Israelis. Yasser Arafat and other Palestine Liberations Organization spokespeople often claimed terrorism was "legitimate armed struggle," a phrase they coined.

Palestinian activists clearly had the opportunity to separate themselves from terrorism with the publishing of a book, yet they instead went out of their way to embrace it. While Palestinian activists claim to be pro-peace on campuses, they, too, justify terrorism as a legitimate act by ignoring the charges or obfuscating the issue. Just the same, when I asked Noura Erakat, "Where were you when S'derot was being bombed?" she said nothing because she couldn't answer why she is silent about the murder of Jews, without showing her undeniably anti-Semitic opinions.

Although the Oslo accords theoretically changed the dynamics on college campuses, much remains the same except that Palestinian activists hide behind the legitimacy of the Palestinian Authority when convenient. Other than names, there is no inherent difference between campus support for the Palestine Liberation Organization prior to the establishment of the Palestinian Authority, and the ISM/PSM today.

Student Dynamics

Over the past twenty years, Jewish student life on campuses has not changed much, yet there have been significant changes for Christians and Muslims. Christian life has grown in strength on campuses, along with a growing number of anti-religious forces. There has even been a growing hostility toward Christian practice, which I see as a symptom of the agenda to remove Christianity from public institutions, while making special allowances for Muslim students so as not to appear anti-Islam. Over the past twenty years though, Muslim students have become increasingly secular and even non-practicing, all of which reflect society. The secularized Muslim students may in some cases pray a few times a day, yet rarely do they attend services at mosques. These Muslim students generally fear not being seen as defenders of the faith by their co-religionists on campus.

This is not the case in Judaism or Christianity. In Islam, not defending the faith makes one an apostate, a charge which no Muslim wants. Defending the faith is central to Islam. When in public therefore, Muslim students, regardless of their level of practice, are therefore compelled to argue with anyone and everyone who disagrees with Islamic religious decrees regarding Israel, in order to not be seen as not defending their faith. I have had wonderfully pleasant conversations with individual Muslims on campuses, but when a second Muslim arrives, the first usually becomes belligerent and antagonistic to not appear soft on Middle East politics. I sometimes avoid these situations because I would much rather have pleasant conversations with people I disagree with, than deal with peer pressure games.

Islamic peer pressure on campuses has always included the intimidation of Jews, an immature tactic, since people who are proud and strong need not minimize others to raise themselves up. I see Palestinians try to intimidate Jewish students on campuses to make them embarrassed to be Jewish and for presumably supporting Israel. Dr. Martin Luther King, Jr. taught people not to fear racist intimidation tactics, a lesson the pro-Israel students must remember.

While walking on the campus of Wayne State University one day, I saw three Muslim women sitting on a concrete bench ahead of me. Before I passed them, I clearly heard one of the women speaking about G-d in English, and when she saw my Kippah after I passed by, the language immediately switched to Arabic with calls of "Wa-Allah" followed by some insults in Arabic about me as a Jew. I quickly realized those three students wanted to intimidate me and most probably bait me into an argument. It became very clear that their verbal assault was automatic; confirming reports from Jewish students who told me they were constantly intimidated by people who knew the Jewish students would understand anti-Semitic slurs in Arabic. I was verbally assaulted once in the five minute walk to my car; I can't imagine how it feels to be a Jewish student on a campus having to hear that several times every day. These situations are why some Jewish students prefer to hide their religion on campus, undoubtedly affecting the rest of their lives. I stood proud because I refuse to be intimidated by anyone, especially weak people with inferiority complexes.

Despite facing these attacks, Jewish student leaders on campuses refuse to be intimidated and are standing tall. Still, these students are troubled because in many cases campus administrators don't care, and even fund anti-Israel events and hate festivals. A single slur against any ethnicity on a campus sparks campus-wide outrage including administrative action, except when Jews and Israel are targeted. The false claims against Jews in general are most prominent in the "Israel Apartheid Week" events, despite the claim being blatantly false. There is a double standard. Open and blatant intimidation of Jews on campuses is acceptable, but a single joke about any other ethnicity, especially Arabs, will likely result in expulsion from a university.

Jewish college students on most campuses are often left to fend for themselves against an onslaught of anti-Semitic propaganda, but they are not alone. There are several great resources for Jewish students, including Betar[1], the

---

1. www.betar.org

Zionist Organization of America[2], Stand with Us[3], Chabad[4], and the Israel on Campus Coalition[5] to name a few.

J Street is a new Jewish organization that is not exactly the pro-Israel organization it portrays itself as. According to an October 2009 article in the *Jerusalem Post*, the Israeli Embassy in Washington, D.C. has let it be known that they do not appreciate J Street's positions on issues. The Israeli Embassy went as far as saying J Street may harm Israel's security interests. J Street's own platform, as posted on their website, calls for "the creation of a viable Palestinian state as part of a negotiated two-state solution, based on the 1967 borders." This is the same plan that Saudi Arabia re-proposed to get around the problem of the Palestinians having to accept a final border agreement, with Israel still existing. The 1967 borders have been termed the "Auschwitz Borders," since they will facilitate the positioning of armies to destroy Israel in hours. These proposed borders leave Israel with a 9-mile corridor which, during wartime, could be cut off easily, thereby destroying Israel's ability to defend itself since resupply and reinforcement capabilities would be eliminated.

In response to J Street, attorney and radio show host Lori Lowenthal Marcus, along with Allyson Rowen Taylor, formerly with StandWithUs.org, co-founded Z Street[6]. With the help of business manager Adrienne Price, blogger-extraordinaire Jerome Gordon and others, Z Street has quickly become a national force. This group takes pride in Israel and Zionism while not giving concessions to terrorists, their supporters, or those hoping for Israel's destruction.

On campuses, Jewish students are always looking for something new for their informational tables, but their real thirst is for organizational help in combating anti-Semitism and the barrage of false divest-from-Israel calls. The divestment campaign started with just that, divestment, and with the Divestment Watch project I was successful in showing it was an illegal boycott, which is why the organizers changed the campaign to Divestment, Boycott, Sanctions, or DBS. Divestment is a form of boycott, and the sanctions that they call for are economic in nature; thus, the campaign has not changed other than in name and is another example of a three-element campaign popularized by Francis Boyle.

2.www.zoa.org
3.www.StandWithUs.org
4.www.chabad.org
5.www.israelcc.org
6.http://www.zstreet.org)

The blatantly false claims that these campaigns will bring peace are the basis for recruiting non-Arab students to the Palestinian side. They slowly ensnare students into their ideology by appealing to the peaceniks who will do anything in the name of peace. These claims also ensnare the rebels who are looking for something to rally behind. The Arabs claim their campaign will force Israel to the negotiating table, but they do not tell the recruits their campaign is illegal and only separates people, because you cannot have peace with someone who would refuse to drink coffee with you. When confronted with these basic points, the peaceniks are usually open to talking about boycotts as an obstacle to peace, but in some cases they have so much pent up emotional energy in support of the divest-from-Israel campaign that they won't give you the time of day. This is exactly what the Palestinians want—to build a future group of adults who will support them no matter what. Most reasonable people will, however, listen to the argument that boycotts never bring people together.

The rebels seldom want to hear the fact that boycotts have never brought peace. These groups include radical Marxists and Trotskyites, who like the idea of dictatorships. These are the same people who will wear Che Guevara T-shirts, but ignore the fact that Che Guevara is a murderer. These same people extol the virtues of murderers like Fidel Castro and Hugo Chavez. They cannot be convinced they are wrong about the Middle East and usually chose to ignore rational discussion. They see the world as potentially utopian and want to place everyone under socialist dictator flags, which is exactly what the Palestinian plan offers: total control of a society. These hypocrites loathe any and all U.S. military involvement in the world, because they do not want to bring democracy anywhere, yet they blame the U.S. for doing nothing in other parts off the world. The problem then grows greater, when the true peaceniks interact with the rebels and create an alliance of people who are comfortable in their one-sided views of the Middle East.

Campuses always have their share of Jews and Arabs who are firm in their beliefs, and the core group of students running events on each side of Middle East politics is usually rather small. The supporters are the people who consist of the vast majority of the members, official or unofficial, and the Arab side only appears to have more support due to the fear Muslims have of not being seen as protecting the faith. Jews, on the other hand, often would rather avoid getting into endless confrontations, which they view as a waste of time. I know I will never persuade an Arab to change his mind about Israel, so I am more than happy to debate only as long I have the time and if there is someone listening who may learn from my words. The goal of the Palestinian side is clearly the destruction of Israel, and I like to prove that to the casual listener. The histories of boycotts and peace make the arguments for me.

The pro-Palestinian side of Middle East politics always loves to bring speakers to campuses, and they get funding from two sources. First, there are student governments that deplore all ethnic hatred except for attacks on Israel. Second, some Arab student groups receive donations funded through various petrol-dollar sources. The Arabs prefer to bring Jewish speakers such as Norm Finkelstein who bash Israel and support the creation of Palestine, because the incongruousness nature of the speaker alone will bring people to hear the speaker and pay ten dollars a ticket. If people think they know what the speaker will say, they probably won't attend unless they are fans of that particular speaker. The same applies on the pro-Israel side. Zionist activists will tell you that it takes a rockstar, so to speak, to bring in people.

College campuses are a major battlefield for the hearts and minds of America as related to future world support for Israel. Jewish students crave for additional community support for campus efforts; they cannot rely on the major cash strapped organizations which are trying to help several campus groups at one time. Local Hillel organizations, for example, will gladly accept donations meant to assist specific campus groups, and they will be happy to help you assist a Jewish camp group of your political or religious liking. Remember: today's students are tomorrow's public opinion. When it comes to campuses, these students are Israel's other IDF and they fight like it. Just as people show their support to groups like Friends of the IDF[7] and Pizza IDF[8], people also need to show their support for Jewish student activism on campuses, be it through the several Jewish organizations on campuses or by offering direct assistance, sponsorship of trips to Israel or on-campus student activities.

7.http://www.israelsoldiers.org
8.http://www.PizzaIDF.org

The Real Rachel Corrie Story

CHAPTER 10

Her story had all the markings of a typical Chicago-land style mafia hit, and then some. Like the Saint Valentine's Day Massacre that preceded it, it too, was designed to send a message: the mafia controlled the city and the news, and nobody in town should dare challenge it. While the police chief spoke strongly against this mob, his deputies would never dare go to work without full armor and a massive show of force. Even construction vehicles needed armor plating.

This was one tough town. There was no effective mayor other than the crime boss, and the people lived in fear. The good ones fled long ago and those who remained either supported the ideology of the mafia, or they lived under the threat of death should they ever leave. They and their children were all stuck there for life and if they ever uttered one bad word about the mafia or the boss, they and their families would be immediately murdered by the same neighbors who had also sworn death oaths.

The gangsters liked getting attention, and they always made sure they blamed their actions on the police chief, a trick they had learned from the days of Al Capone. Gangster cells would compete against each other for the respect of their boss, peers and to move ahead, yet none acted without approval of the boss. One such cell wanted to get the attention of the world, but how? Its previous hits against the regional town's people did not receive the kind of media attention it desired. The gangsters needed a new plan to stay on top and soon ideas emerged, the best of which was to murder a cute blonde foreigner and blame the police chief.

They knew the law: If they locked a girl in the trunk of a car which was going to be crushed in a junk yard, they themselves were legally responsible for the murder, not the junk yard owner nor the junk yard employees who would do the actual crushing, despite being at the switch.

Knowingly fooling the junk yard would certainly obfuscate the actual crime, but only if they could control the media and media access to the scene. They knew they controlled the town so nobody would be prosecuted, so blaming the junk yard would be easy, especially with hometown media help; thus they could once again make the police chief look bad. It was a win-win for the mafia, and if they milked it in the media, people would eventually believe the lie and perpetuate the story to their advantage. The plan was set.

This is the real and tragic story of Rachel Corrie, the young blonde American student who wanted to do the right thing by helping the underdog, the same people who eventually murdered her on March 16, 2003. Rachel was recruited to join the divest-from-Israel movement, and that is where the deception and media lies began.

Rachel was first told that boycotting Israel would effectively bring Israel to its knees at the negotiating table with the Palestinians, but that is neither the truth nor the reason behind the divest-from-Israel campaign. Rachel didn't know the Arab boycott actually began in 1921, twenty-seven years before Israel was established as a way to starve out the Jews before they could create a Jewish state, nor did she know that the Arab league was formed to oversee the boycott which still exists today. Rachel was never told the only Arab country that no longer adheres to the boycott is Jordan, as trade is building a growing peace between the two nations and Jordan's economy is growing quickly as a result.

The Palestinians continually fail to mention the warmongering effects of their boycott, when recruiting students such as Rachel Corrie to join their cause. This young and impressionable girl traveled to Palestinian areas where she was, as the Arabs admit, recruited to help block an Israeli bulldozer from tearing down the home of a Palestinian terrorist. When such protests happen, people usually stand in front of a building in plain sight so oncoming wrecking crews can see them. In this case, however, Rachel was strategically hidden behind a pile of dirt. It is likely that she was restrained against her will or rendered unconscious, because otherwise she would have moved away as a natural reaction. Because of her location, the oncoming bulldozer operator had no way of seeing or hearing her, which resulted in her unfortunate death.

Who is to blame? If a person is forced or even tricked to be in a position against her will, the law calls that kidnapping. If a person subsequently dies due to being in a position where she was knowingly placed in harm's way, that is defined as murder and the guilt is placed on the people who put her in that position, just as it would be in the junk yard example. Here, the blame squarely rests upon Rachel's so-called Palestinian "friends" who had her murdered in a classic mafia-style hit in order to make Israel look bad.

Every year on the anniversary of her death, Arabs and ignorant, pro-boycott sympathizers lie to people that Rachel was a victim of "Israeli aggression." In reality, Rachel was the victim of gangsters who purposely continue to blame others for their own actions. They set up a young innocent woman to die for the political gain of others.

I can see past the gangster-terrorist lies. I know Islamic fascist Arabs murdered Rachel in order to further their hate-filled agenda to destroy Israel by recrimination and terrorism. I mourn her murder every March 16th in the same way I mourn the murder of other victims of Arab terrorism, and I will not fall for libelous PR claims by terrorists and their supporters.

The Flotilla Façade

CHAPTER 11

It quickly became known as the "Gaza Flotilla" when the news broke on television stations across the world. The news moved so fast that I wondered if the press releases were ready go in advance, since video cameras were in place to create television show quality results. As it turns out, I was right: it was a staged media event. Rather than telling the story from the beginning about what happened on May 31, 2010, I will first show how the stage was set for the audience, thereby giving away the magician's secrets.

The Republic of Turkey was founded in 1923 from the remnants of the defeated Ottoman Empire. Turkey is a parliamentary democracy with an elected President and civil law system derived from various European continental systems. It is an Islamic nation with cordial diplomatic relations with Israel, yet such relations have lately been strained with the election of radical Islamist leaders. Here is where the story begins.

About ten days before the flotilla event, Turkey informed Israel it was sending a flotilla of ships with "humanitarian" aid to Gaza, with the specific intent of violating and breaking the joint Israel-Egypt blockade. This Gaza blockade was neither random nor meant as punishment as Hamas supports have claimed, but rather it was created in response to the threat the Hamas government in Gaza imposes to both Israel and Egypt. Egypt enforces the blockade in the south of Gaza, though Israel detractors generally neglect that point or even to mention Egypt at all in their criticism. Ignoring Egypt helps build the public illusion that Israel is the oppressor of all Arabs around the world. They also neglect to say that Egypt is in fear of the growing radical Islamists who wish to topple their government and create another radical Islamic state like Syria and Iran.

Israel responded by warning Turkey not to send the ships directly to Gaza, but to instead send them to Israeli ports where the goods could be offloaded from the ships, placed on trucks, and sent to Gaza over land the way Israel and Egypt both send humanitarian aid to Gaza daily. Israel and Egypt make sure food, clothing, medicine and utility services are in ample supply in Gaza. Goods that can be used to make bombs, missiles and reinforced bomb shelters are not allowed. Construction supplies are generally allowed in, but not concrete, which can be used to create reinforced military shelters.

The image of Gaza being a world of rubble is a planned media show, reinforced by the media which is limited as to where they can go and what they can tape. There is no freedom in Gaza, thanks to Hamas, which remains dangerous for the press. The kidnapping of reporter Steve Centanni of Fox News in 2006 was far from unique and sent a message to reporters: report what Hamas wants you to report or else. After his release, Steve said he thought he was going to be killed on several occasions and is lucky to be alive. This is why journalists have to be very careful when reporting in Arab areas, including Gaza, resulting in a forced anti-Israel slant. Personally, I would rather see footage from reporters and networks with integrity, who will not report in places where they are not free to independently report. Unfortunately, the business of news makes being on the scene a necessity; thus, we are often stuck with distorted news.

The flotilla set sail and stopped at Cypress before heading to Gaza. Israel and the world were told the ships were filled with peace activists, which Israel had no reason to doubt. At first, Israel tried to get the ships to divert to Israeli ports, but that failed, forcing Israel to act accordingly. The world would later criticize Israel for responding with excess force, which was simply not true. When Israeli commandos boarded the ships to block them from entering Gaza, they carried paintball guns to act as riot control, as opposed to a full blown military response. This was Israel's mistake. The soldiers were essentially defenseless and were assaulted by the alleged peace activists who attacked them with pipes, knives and other weapons far superior to paintball guns. Video was released showing the Israeli boarding party being beaten with lead pipes and tossed overboard. Israel, therefore, had no choice but to respond to deadly force with deadly force. Its boarding of the ships was legal under international law, as is defending ones self using deadly force to counter deadly force. What Israel did not realize was that they were the victims of an elaborate hoax.

First, real peace activists do not use violence. We later learned that Hamas activists ran this ship. Ha'aretz[1], as one of Israel's leading newspapers, published an article on June 6, 2010, "IDF: Five Gaza flotilla activists linked to Hamas, Al-Qaida." The article stated, "One of the activists exposed by the IDF was named as Iranian-born Fatima Mahmadi, a 31-year-old resident of the United States. According to the IDF, Mohammadi is a member of Viva Palestine, a movement that had tried bringing illegal electronic devices into the Gaza Strip."

The Ha'aretz article mentioned one other person who is of particular interest: "Ken O'Keefe, a 41-year-old citizen of the United States and Britain, another activist named by the IDF as having links to terrorist organizations. According to the IDF, O'Keefe is an extremist who hates Israel and whose 'goal was to reach Gaza in order to help train and establish Hamas commando units.'"

---

1. www.haaretz.com

Also aboard the Mavi Marmara ship was Jamal Elshayyal, a reporter for Al-Jazeera Television, who reported live with a cameraman.[2] A video of the live report was posed on youtube.com by Al Jazeera English.[3] You are right to wonder why a news crew would be aboard a humanitarian ship, since delivering food to Gaza where food is abundant is not news. There had to be another reason to have a news crew on the ship.

First, Al Jazeera clearly expected to take footage of Israelis boarding the ships. Had the news been the ship breaking the blockade by docking in Gaza, the Al-Jazeera English Television News would have reported this from the shores of Gaza. This is akin to the crab fishing shows on cable television. Had the interesting part of those shows been the arrival of the crabs at the dock, there would be no need for a camera crew to be aboard the ships. The news in both cases is what would happen on the ships, thereby indicating Al Jazeera knew of the plan in advance and even brought satellite broadcasting equipment along to report the planned Arab violence against Israel, live. This was also not an attempt to create a documentary. The crab fishing programs tape the footage for later editing. There had to be additional Al Jazeera staff on board to run the satellite equipment, including technicians and a producer. No network would bring all that equipment and staff unless they knew something big would happen, which Al-Jazeera did.

Second, the ship was very well and evenly illuminated. The lighting on the ships deck is television lighting, which is much brighter than normal lighting and especially brighter than any ship would have, since it consumes a large amount of electricity. The video clearly shows video lighting. The ship's deck was a floating television studio. Further proof of this is not only was the interior lighting different, but also the lighting in another part of the deck was dimmer, indicating a completely different lighting schema. Israel did not just board a ship; Israeli soldiers entered a television studio and unwittingly became the stars of a show.

Israel was set up and fell for a trap in which it would have lost either way. Allowing ships with unknown cargo could have allowed heavy weapons into Gaza, which could have resulted in the murder of Israelis by way of more rocket launches from Gaza. Israel walked into a trap taped by a television

2.http://www.youtube.com/watch?v=xFEBbDkyrqQ
3.http://www.youtube.com/user/AlJazeeraEnglish

crew from the one network Hamas supports. Building the media circus, one of the ships that sailed later was named the Rachel Corrie, which of course is the direct link between the flotilla and the Israel boycott campaign which uses Rachel as the poster child to attack Israel.

Here is where Ken O'Keefe fits into the picture. The former U.S. Marine claims Israeli soldiers aboard the ship had beaten him. As the Ha'aretz report states, "O'Keefe is an extremist who hates Israel and whose 'goal was to reach Gaza in order to help train and establish Hamas commando units.'" O'Keefe was the perfect foil. His stated goal was to train Hamas commando units, so if Hamas really wanted him for that, they would have welcomed him into Gaza at a border crossing, which of course, did not happen. If he had died in the Hamas televisions show, they would have had another Rachel Corrie on their hands. Only this time, they would broadcast the death of a former U.S. Marine, which would undoubtedly raise significant American ire against Israel. Hamas therefore wanted O'Keefe to die aboard the ship as he would be more valuable to Hamas dead as a media tool. In a June 4, 2010, television interview[4], the injuries to O'Keefe were slash cuts to his face, which are not injuries Israeli soldiers could have inflicted with paint ball guns. The slash marks were radiating from a single forehead bruise in a branch like pattern, as if from an object with chains attached to the end. That is not a weapon Israel uses, but rather fits the patterns of an improvised pipe weapon, which matches Hamas' on-board arsenal. This makes me believe O'Keefe was struck in the head from above by an Arab with a medieval mace-type weapon, because the Arabs wanted him to die. Hamas wanted another Rachel Corrie, but they failed to kill O'Keefe.

The ship was clearly not filled with peace activists as they claimed; rather, it was filled with Hamas activists who wanted to murder Jews and destroy Israel. The Gaza flotilla was clearly a public relations vehicle to embarrass Israel.

O'Keefe stated he wanted to train Hamas commandos. Had these been peace activist ships, they would have never allowed him and others aboard. Had this been a peace ship, the occupants would have never attacked soldiers boarding the ship with pipes and knives. And, in case you were wondering, it is

4.http://pulsemedia.org/2010/06/06/ken-okeefe-we-the-defenders-of-the-mavi-marmara/

generally not healthy to attack soldiers, because they will fight back and bring an army with them.

Israel's response

The Monday morning after the Gaza flotilla raid, Israeli Deputy Foreign Minister Danny Ayalon held a press conference in which he stated:

> I want to report this morning that the armada of hate and violence in support of the Hamas terror organization was a premeditated and outrageous provocation. The organizers are well known for their ties to global Jihad, Al-Qaeda and Hamas. They have a history of arms smuggling and deadly terror. On board the ship we found weapons prepared in advance and used against our forces.
>
> The organizers' intent was violent, their method was violent, and the results were unfortunately, violent. Israel regrets any loss of life and did everything to avoid this outcome. We repeatedly called upon the organizers, and all those who associated with them, through diplomatic channels and any other means we could, to stop this provocation. The so-called humanitarian aid was not for a humanitarian purpose. Had it been for a humanitarian purpose, they would have accepted our offer to deliver all humanitarian supplies through the appropriate channels which are used on a daily basis, as we make sure that Gaza will not be short of humanitarian supplies. On a daily basis we do that.
>
> We asked them to send [the supplies] through the proper channels, whether it's the UN, whether it's the Red Cross, whether it's our people, but to no avail. In fact, what they said was, that it's a humanitarian campaign, but they said, repeatedly, that their intent and purpose was to break the maritime blockade on Gaza. The maritime blockade on Gaza is very legal and justified by the terror that Hamas is applying in Gaza. Allowing these ships to go in a illegal way to Gaza would

have opened a corridor of smuggling arms and terrorists to Gaza with the inevitable results of many, many thousands of civilian deaths, and violence all over the area.

After these repeated calls were not heeded by the organizers, we told them that they will not be allowed to break the blockade. As according to maritime law we have the right to do that. Unfortunately, the people and organizers on the ship did not heed the calls of our forces this morning to peacefully follow them and bring a peaceful closure to this event.

No sovereign country would tolerate such violence against its civilian population, against its sovereignty, against international law. And we in Israel call today upon all relevant parties and on all relevant countries to work together in calming the situation.

Thank you very much.

The Turkish Response

After the incident, The Republic of Turkey publicly complained to Israel, as if they had no idea what was going to happen. This is absurd, considering the conversations the two nations had prior to the flotilla boarding, and since Turkey did not disclose the real nature of the ships sailing under their flag, which they had requested Israel to allow. That explains the circuitous route the ships took, thus giving Turkey plausible denial. Israel remained silent in order to not create a diplomatic crisis between the two nations.

Turkey was clearly trying to add fuel to the firestorm. Israel could have stated the obvious in response—that Turkey lied—but wisely chose to calm the situation by just not commenting. Israel was not interested in engaging in a diplomatic fight that was against both nations' interests. Israel's silence was a move toward preserving peace.

In reviewing the Gaza flotilla case, people should ask themselves if they think a Hamas terrorist flotilla, masked as peace mission, really advances peace, or if it is yet another obstacle to peace. If the intention were really peaceful and humanitarian in nature, they would not have needed to build the elaborate hoax. They could have simply sent the cargo by land through Israeli ports; but they didn't, which proves it was all an elaborate show to get people to hate Israel.

Princess Cruise Lines Boycott Based on False Information

It did not take long for the Israel haters to further capitalize on the flotilla façade. An opportunity knocked on their door the next day, and the Israel haters created another hoax, just like the fake Nike show ad. Again, Israel, as justified by international law, had boarded the flotilla of ships early on May 31, 2010, to enforce its and Egypt's joint blockade.

At the time of the incident, Princess Cruises had a passenger ship heading to Israel as part of their regular seasonal Holy Land Cruises, which have been an active part of their business for more than twenty years. As are many itineraries in the cruise industry, it is seasonal, operates between May and November, and has ten such cruises scheduled for 2010. The tour starts with Italy and makes stops in religiously significant places in Croatia, Egypt, Turkey, Greece, and two stops in Israel.[5]

The following email was circulated soon after:

> Subject: PRINCESS CRUISE LINES
> Email content:
> WE MUST BOYCOTT THIS CRUISE LINE. JEWS TAKE CRUISES FREQUENTLY, AND WE MUST SHOW THEM THAT THEIR WALLETS WILL SUFFER BY DOING THIS TO US.
> SHOULD WE USE PRINCESS CRUISE LINES ANYMORE LIKE WATCHING MEL GIBSON MOVIES ANYMORE SINCE HIS COMMENTS ABOUT HIS FAMILY AGAINST JEWS

5.http://www.princess.com/find/itineraryDetails.do?subnav=true&voyageCode=K007&tourCode=&resType=C&departurePort=&noOfCruiseDays=&noOfTourDays=&travelOrder=&bID=PCPB&airPortCode=&port=VCE&productCode=EHB120&departureDate=Jun+20%2C+2010&productDesc=Holy+Land%3A+Venice+to+Athens+-+12+Days

Subject: PRINCESS CRUISE LINES

Date: Thursday, June 3, 2010, 10:45 AM

Yesterday, 6/2/2010, the Pacific Princess, carrying 700 passengers, canceled a stop at Ashdod, Israel. Instead, they informed the passengers they would stop in Egypt as an alternative. Princess is now bowing to pressure and boycotting Israel. Please pass this on to all Jewish Americans to let them know that there are alternatives to Princess. Thank you.

Susan Rosenbluth, Editor and Publisher of *The Jewish Voice and Opinion*, pointed out the email is a hoax, and the wording proves it. Let's examine the specific wording of the email, both the original and embellishments in capital letters.

First is the line "JEWS TAKE CRUISES FREQUENTLY." The wording is not 'we take' or anything to the effect of being inclusive. Second, the words "BY DOING THIS TO US" is very reminiscent of the wording Arabs use when complaining about Israel and Jews. Third, the grammar in the second paragraph is rather awkward, indicating it did not come from a native English speaker. Fourth, the last paragraph is dated June 2, the day the ship was supposed to dock in Israel. While it is possible for that email to have been circulated that same day, it is full of misinformation, indicating this writer, who is clearly different from the first writer, did not know the facts of the case whatsoever.

In fairness to Princess Cruises, the following is their response to the boycott call.

News Article

6/8/2010

Statement on Cruise Calls to Israel

In response to recent inquiries, we would like to clarify why we cancelled the Pacific Princess' call to Ashdod, Israel on June 2. The ship did call at Haifa, Israel the previous day on June 1.

Just two days prior to our scheduled call to Ashdod, a violent incident occurred between the Israeli Defense Forces and a flotilla of ships carrying aid to the Gaza Strip. This unfortunate event resulted in several fatalities.

Upon careful review of the situation and information provided by the U.S. State Department and other sources, we were concerned about potential violence in reaction to the incident. Our decision, which was not politically motivated, was made in the best interest of the safety and security of our passengers and crew.

Pacific Princess is scheduled to call in Israel at the end of June, and we expect to maintain the published itinerary. However, as with all of our ports of call, we continuously monitor information that may affect our ships' routings. Should a decision be made to make any adjustments, affected passengers would be advised as soon as possible.

I contacted Julie Benson, Vice President for Public Relations at Princess Cruises, and asked some very tough questions to get to the facts. For starters, the fact that the ship did not stop in Ashdod is correct. The day after the flotilla raid, the Pacific Princess ship was docked in Haifa where the passengers reportedly had, as expected, a wonderful and safe excursion. That day though, the flotilla news was centered on Ashdod, which is where the flotilla ships were taken and arrests were made. Ashdod was the center of international news and there were concerns, including those from Israeli police, of potential violence. The Pacific Princess ship was scheduled to be in the Ashdod port the following day, June 2, a fact which understandably created security concerns for the cruise ship company. The fact is nobody knew what was going to happen next.

Princess Cruises, like every good company, is concerned with the safety and welfare of their customers. They were scheduled to arrive in the Ashdod port, and naturally started to ask experts if they felt Ashdod was safe the next morning. After consulting with Israeli police and cruise line security staff based in Israel, they decided to skip Ashdod in this one cruise only in order to play it safe. Let's face it—any complaints about skipping the one port of call would be better than having to deal with potential liability issues after the fact; thus, the company acted prudently.

The boycott claim says the cruise line should be boycotted because they are complying with the Arab boycott of Israel, but that is not true. The cruise line cancelled one port of call on one trip and then continued on to their next port of call for that itinerary, which is Egypt. The change in their itinerary is actually part of their policy and in the contract every passenger signs.

In the contract, the term "Carrier" means "Princess Cruises" and the contract states:

3. NOTICE CONCERNING SAFETY AND SECURITY.

Carrier visits a large number of ports in numerous countries around the world. At any given moment there are likely to be "trouble spots" in the world in terms of war, terrorism, crime, Act of God, civil commotions, labor trouble, and/or other potential sources of harm. Local conditions and infrastructure may also create hazards to Passengers while off the ship. Accordingly, it may be necessary to change, cancel or terminate the scheduled cruise or any activities related to the cruise, including without limitation shore excursions and port visits. Although Carrier endeavors to provide reasonable protection for Your comfort and safety onboard its ships, Carrier cannot guarantee freedom from all risks associated with war, terrorism, crime or other potential sources of harm. Carrier reminds all Passengers that they must ultimately assume responsibility for their actions while ashore. The United States Department of State and other similar government agencies regularly issue advisories and warnings to travelers giving details of local conditions in specified cities and countries according to such agency's perception of risks to travelers. Carrier strongly recommends that Passengers and their travel agents obtain and consider such information when making travel decisions.

Princess Cruises, therefore, acted without regard to politics, for what they saw as a potential safety concern. While some people may not agree with their judgment call, it was just that. More importantly, subsequent cruises will continue to make the scheduled two stops in Israel, which is a popular destination. The cruise line is not taking part in the Arab boycott as claimed; thus, the call to boycott Princess Cruises is unfounded. It is another case of a fraudulent boycott by Arabs that is designed to get Jews to boycott companies friendly to Israel, in order to get Jews to help fulfill dream of the Arab boycott being used to destroy Israel.

Flotilla of the Bands

Perhaps one of the biggest peace activism frauds being perpetrated is the movement to get musicians to boycott performance in Israel. While some musical groups have boycotted Israel in the past, the flotilla incident created a new excuse to recruit more bands to join. One of the greatest advantages of being a famous actor or musician is the ability to use that fame to press his own political and social causes. Still, he must act responsibility to make sure his own credibility is not being abused or manipulated.

When artists are recruited to boycott performing in Israel, I doubt they are being told that having an Israeli stamp in their passports will preclude them from entering most Arab states. When working at the research laboratories at Sherwin Williams, I spoke with sales professionals in the International Group and asked about the passport dilemma. They explained that they request special "temporary passports" for their trips to Arab countries, thus allowing them access into the Arab nations, since their regular passports have Israeli stamps. I then asked about travel to Israel after having a new passport with an Arab nation stamp inside. I was told Israel will ask questions, as they do with everyone, but it is not a major problem. I doubt, therefore, musicians are told Israel does not restrict entry based on passport stamps.

The basic discrimination based on passport stamps should be the real issue for the performers and everyone else, and in many cases it is. The fact is, most Arab nations discriminate against anyone who has Israel stamped in their passports; Israel does not discriminate against those with Arab stamps. That should be the focus of bands who wish to bring peace and equality to the Middle East.

Israel is a popular destination for many bands for several reasons. First, as Bret Stephens, Foreign-Affairs Columnist for the Wall Street Journal, pointed out on Shalom TV, Israel is the most inclusive society in the Middle East[6]. Israel is the only country in the region that protects gay rights, including the rights of homosexuals to openly serve in the military. Israel is the only nation in the Middle East that affords women's rights in society. While corruption is overlooked in Arab dictatorships, Israeli politicians are held to the same justice standards as the citizens. Israel is also the only nation in the region which allows artists the right to offend. Unlike in Arab nations, musicians are not censored in Israel. The fact is, Israel is the only nation in the Middle East which upholds the very same rights that the boycotting bands are espousing with their boycott. By boycotting Israel, these bands are blaming the people they should be supporting.

At the same time, few of these bands would be able to perform in Arab states due to Islamic censorship of their lyrics, thus CD sales. So-called "moderate" nations such as Saudi Arabia would probably not let these bands enter their countries. These bands probably do not realize that they are not being booked in Arab nations due to censorship. The bands that do perform in Arab nations, not that I can name any, surely face travel restrictions and must undertake major security precautions.

The boycotting bands have fallen for the false claim that boycotting brings peace, when the opposite is true. If these bands really want peace, they should insist on performing in both Israel and Arab countries without passport stamp restrictions, without censorship, and with freedom of travel. Freedom of travel exists in Israel, but not in Arab nations for a reason—Arab dictators do not want foreigners to see the oppressed Arab poor, while the oil-baron kings live in complete opulence. Israel, on the other hand, has nothing to hide.

Bands that boycott Israel by canceling performance dates are not only engaging the illegal Arab boycott of Israel, but they are furthering the separation of people, the opposite of what their peace desires are. These bands are

6.http://www.youtube.com/watch?v=UN-JJreC4JQ

inherently providing aid and comfort to nations sworn to Israel's destruction. By boycotting Israel, these bands are not just furthering the Arab boycott; they are making a public statement against peace in the Middle East. Bands taking stances in favor of free performance are the true seekers of peace in the Middle East.

Divest from Israel
Hate-fests

CHAPTER 12

 n his article "The Socialism of Fools: The Left, the Jews and Israel," Dr. Seymour Martin Lipset wrote:

> Shortly before he was assassinated, Martin Luther King, Jr., was in Boston on a fund-raising mission, and I had the good fortune to attend a dinner which was given for him in Cambridge...One of the young men present happened to make some remark

against the Zionists. Dr. King snapped at him and said, "Don't talk like that! When people criticize Zionists, they mean Jews. You're talking anti-Semitism!" [1]

On campuses across the country, events promoting divesting and boycotting Israel are so common that they hardly raise an eyebrow anymore in the local Jewish communities surrounding those campuses. Most Jews have become apathetic to these events, yet ironically, refer to them as isolated incidents. Unfortunately, some people do not realize these events are designed to build future generations of Israel-haters that go beyond on-campus protesters. The following are three examples of what is happening on campuses nationally, where being anti-Israel is a code for publicly expressing anti-Semitism and getting away with it.

Ohio State

I kept my face off of the Boycott Watch website for many years because I was not interested in the publicity; I just wanted to get the truth out. Anonymity came in handy when I created Divestment Watch to monitor the divest-from-Israel campaign specifically. Divestment is a form of boycotting, and the campaign is part of the greater Arab boycott of Israel. I knew that if I wanted to attend the Divestment from Israel conferences, I was better off not being recognized, but I was still generally recognizable by my photograph from my hard-hitting articles, especially those about divesting from Israel, and countless media appearances when I ran the campaign to deport the Nazi John "Ivan the Terrible" Demjanjuk. I was especially concerned I would be recognized and banned from attending the divest-from-Israel conferences, so I decided to go undercover to one such conference at Ohio State University on November 7-9, 2004.

When I registered, I purposely scribbled my name illegibly; however, I was caught off guard when asked for identification for the registration. I replied that I was a reporter, keep my home address confidential, and I just showed them a homemade business card. I was very surprised they accepted that, especially with a police officer at the registration table.

1.*Encounter* magazine, December, 1969 (page 24)

One of my key objectives at that conference was to determine the involvement of Professor Francis Boyle, the founder of the divest-from-Israel movement. Boyle's name was not on the event literature, website or schedule, but the wording throughout the event clearly indicated his direct involvement. I was certain the event organizers, along with most of the presenters, knew about Boyle. I figured if the registration desk people knew who Boyle was and his connection to the divest-from-Israel movement, it would both indicate the level of involvement all the event staff had with him and his active participation with the divest-from-Israel campaign. I asked if he were attending and was very surprised at the nonchalant "he didn't make it in" response, which clearly indicated his not only active participation, but their complete familiarity with him. Perhaps that is why my registration without identification was instantly accepted. I knew the secret name; thus, they thought I was in their camp. I soon discovered though, that as a reporter I was barred from attending the breakout sessions, which were meant to plan and coordinate campus activities nationally. Regardless, just sitting in the main room and taking notes that Sunday was shocking enough.

There were about 100 attendees at the conference, half of whom I believe were more interested in what was happening, than in participating in the divest-from-Israel movement. Outside the main entrance, there were three protests groups in a small area fenced off by the police: the Betar Zionist youth group of which I am affiliated, the Protest Warriors who are Christian activists, and Rabbi Avi Weiss leading his Amcha/Coalition for Jewish Concerns group. All together, there were far more anti-divestment protesters and spectators at that conference than actual divest-from-Israel advocates.

While the Ohio State weekend event had all the Israel bashing you could imagine and then some, it had one presentation that single-handedly demonstrated proof that the conference was a complete anti-Semitic hate-fest designed to vilify all Jews. Stokely Carmichael, a.k.a. Kwame Ture, was a 1960s Black Panther leader whom I had never paid any attention to before that day; though I had heard he was an anti-Semite. Although he claimed to be nonviolent as head of the Student Nonviolent Coordinating Committee or "SNiCC," he joined and became a leader of the Black Panther Party that had once marched into the California state capital fully armed. The Black Panthers had deadly confrontations with police officers, which hardly made them nonviolent.

The Ohio State divest-from-Israel conference organizers showed everyone a video tape of Carmichael delivering a speech about Zionism and Jews. This footage was so full of historical inaccuracies that it would take an entire book to cover them all. Carmichael just kept ranting and throwing out gratuitous statements, all of which were nothing more than a rant of non sequiturs. In the video, for example, Carmichael stated, "Judaism has nothing to do with Zionism." Of course, this is complete nonsense, because the Bible constantly refers to Zion as both the location of the Holy Temple of Judaism and a synonym for the city of Jerusalem. Separating Jerusalem from Judaism is like separating Washington, D.C. from the United States—it makes no sense. Stokely Carmichael also stated, "Judaism and Zionism must be completely separated." This comment diametrically opposes what Dr. King once said: "Don't talk like that! When people criticize Zionists, they mean Jews. You're talking anti-Semitism!"

Carmichael also stated, "If you will look through at all religions, the majority of them, they all have a theme running through them which say that to be redeemed one must suffer.... The thing of Judaism is that the Jews must suffer—suffer for humanity." In this statement, he clearly and irresponsibly advocated making Jews suffer to advance his revolutionary view of the world.

Carmichael has long been an irrelevant footnote in history, which adds to the question of why did the organizers show the video of his speech on the first place? Were they not any better spokespeople available, either live or on video? After all, Carmichael claimed to be nonviolent, yet he advocated violence. Even the name of his organization, the Black Panthers, gives the impression of violence. In his own words, Carmichael proves he was philosophically against the nonviolent approach of Dr. King. The reason the video was shown, therefore, could have only been because the divest-from-Israel conference organizers wanted to both promote the hatred of Jews and advocate or justify violence against Jews. Had the organizers of the Ohio State University event wanted peace and coexistence, they would have never considered showing the video of Carmichael. Sadly, only the Jews who were protesting the event bothered challenging these hate-videos. The event organizers and presenters acted as if the venom they were presenting was like saying one plus one equals two. That is just one reason why I call the divest-from-Israel conferences what they are: unabashed hate-fests.

This was the same conference where I had interviewed Adam Shapiro, who presented a very cold personality. I also spoke to a few of the student attendees, all of whom gave me the impression that they were really not sure why they were boycotting Israel other than their friends were involved, or as one participant stated. "It sounded like a good to do." I then managed to speak to one of the event organizers in the hallway. In the middle of her unsure statements, one of her friends interrupted, asking her to go somewhere, and she excused herself. Back in the main room, I asked one of the video present-ers for a copy of the Carmichael video; they had promised me one, but never delivered.

Before the Ohio State event, I had written to the university president about my many concerns with the school's essentially advocating hate toward Jews and the illegal nature of foreign sanctioned boycotts, yet received no reply. The content of the conference proved my fears were well-founded. The Ohio State hate-fest conclusively proved Arab students were recruiting Americans to join the Arab boycott under false pretenses. It was an on-campus hate-fest and partially funded by taxpayer dollars! Several articles were written about the Ohio State Hate-fest, and although I had hoped to see a letter of regret from the University for hosting the event, I saw no such comments whatsoever.

Georgetown

I did not attend the divest-from-Israel hate-fest at Rutgers in 2005, but by the time the Palestine Solidarity Movement hate-fest was held at Georgetown University in Washington, DC on February 17-19, 2006, I had a well known reputation for fighting divestment, especially with organizers of such events. I knew that if I went, I would have to go deep under cover again. I had real media credentials, thanks to a magazine, which I used because I knew I was the one person they did not want at their event. I had already filed complaints to the U.S. Department of Commerce about the hate-fests and other divest-from-Israel campaigns being illegal boycotts, which the divestment conference organizers knew. Thanks to my extensive writing and other work on the topic, Internet search engines consistently brought up the Divestment Watch website in the top three search results for the word 'divestment.' More importantly, I was the person who originated the argument about the divest-from-Israel campaign being illegal foreign boycotts, anti-Semitic and anti-peace; thus, I was already known as the expert on the topic. The simple fact is the analysis I presented in my articles predate the arguments in every other publication, and the first people to use my arguments did so almost verbatim. I am proud to be the person who first created the anti-divestment campaign and am happy when others use my work. Although it does not happen often, I hope to receive proper credit when for my work when it is used.

One person I wish could have attended the Georgetown hate-fest was Jerry Gordon, whom I met on the phone when preparing for the conference. Jerry was unable to attend at the last minute, but I kept in contact with him regarding the event, and we keep in touch to this day. Jerry is a very insightful writer and soft-spoken radio commentator who makes people think. My close friend Mikhail Alterman joined me at this conference, and we worked alone so as to not draw attention to either one of us. I was very surprised that one person I knew openly attended as himself, Lee Kaplan, as he had written many negative articles about the divestment organizers. I sat next to Lee, whom I originally met at the Ohio State University hate-fest two years prior, in one of the Georgetown sessions and gave him considerable grief about his choice of cigars so that nobody would think we were friends.

Lee summed up why the divest-from-Israel advocates welcomed him to the conference. In response to a snide comment, Lee said, "Hey, I've given you lots of publicity. You should be paying me to be here" to the presenters of the session. Lee is bold and brash, and he was careful not to blow my cover.

I attended a few breakout sessions and one in particular caught my attention: "Christian Outreach—A Moral Call to Action." The title alone sounded interesting. It was presented by Nadeem Muaddi of Temple University Students for Justice in Palestine and Maher Bitar of Georgetown University Students for Justice in Palestine, both Muslim, but their presentation had nothing to do with morality.

The session started with a photo projected at the front of the room depicting what they claimed were two "Israeli soldiers" blocking an elderly Christian woman who was carrying a cross and rosary beads from attending church. This obviously professional and staged photo had one little problem—the two "Israeli soldiers" were each carrying a World War II era replica M3 submachine gun, which was also known as the grease gun, a weapon Israel has not used since about 1949. Most people would have just assumed the soldiers were carrying Uzi's because of some rudimentary design similarities, but anyone who has studied military history could see those guns were not even good replicas. This was clear anti-Semitic incitement since it was specifically staged to evoke angry sentiment toward Israel by falsely depicting Jews as anti-Christian. To these Muslims, I immediately realized that "Christian Outreach—A Moral Call to Action" meant making immoral claims to get Christians to hate Jews.

I did not remain silent. During the question and answer portion of the program, I asked the presenters to put the photo back on the screen, which they did. I then asked the University appointed monitor to take note. I pointed out why the photo was an obvious forgery in front of everyone and then asked, "If you are willing to professionally produce this obvious forgery, why should we believe anything else you have said here today?" The reaction from the audience was mixed, but the presenters looked like deer in headlights. They did not answer my question, but instead ended the session immediately. That fake photo miraculously and almost instantly vanished from all divest-from-Israel websites—they obviously realized I had caught them in a lie.

Attended by a few other undercover Jewish activists that I recognized, the session about Christian outreach was not what I expected. I thought I was going to hear about recruitment techniques, but numerous Muslims told the packed room with about seventy-five attendees how they should infiltrate churches even if they do not believe in Christianity, and lie to priests, ministers and reverends to get their confidence. Session attendees were told to dress up for church by wearing dresses and suits to play the part of good wholesome Christians, including covering up any tattoos. The Muslim presenters told their audience to act as if they were true Christian believers and instructed them to resume their normal activities after their church infiltrations. After time, they were told that they could then ask for rooms in the churches to present their divest-from-Israel campaigns to other church members and that they would receive free rooms for events which, with the cover of the church, would give them instant credibility. Yes, Muslims were telling Christians to lie to their clergy, and it was done as an official part of the divest-from-Israel conferences, which further illustrates this event was another hate-fest. This explains the forged photo at the opening of the session. The lie of Jews preventing Christians from prayer was the perfect prelude to their presentation. The campaign organizers not only wanted to present a justification for what they were about to present, but they also wanted to make sure their Christians audience was comfortable in lying to their clergy. It was perhaps the single worst case of religious disrespect I have ever personally witnessed. It was a case of Muslims wanting to use Christians to do their dirty work against Jews. This whole scene is reminiscent of classic 1970s American Neo-Nazi hate-messages with hateful recordings such as, "This is Adolf Eichmann... Attention white Christians. The Jew is using the Nigger as muscle against you." Only this time it was Muslims inciting Christians against Jews. What a world.

Further illustrating the anti-Semitic nature of the presentations, Nadeem Muaddi said, "Targeting civilians is immoral, but all Israelis are in the Army Reserves." This statement is a clear call and justification to physically attack all Israelis, and yet another example of the "legitimate armed struggle" that his organization called for in their own book. Nadeem told his audience that Israelis are all legitimate targets of terrorism, which is part of the "legitimate armed struggle" claim. This was a further call to violence, yet the monitor said nothing.

To these people, it does not matter who is in uniform and who is not because, as Nadeem stated, "All Israelis are in the Army Reserves." This is the same exact reasoning and claim that terrorists make when explaining why they murder people in pizza shops and discotheques indiscriminately. If all Jews are soldiers, then even a mother and her infant child are legitimate targets of terrorism, according to the terrorists and the ISM/PSM. This sick and twisted justification for terrorism is not just limited to Israel as targets. The terrorist attacks on the September 11, 2001, were aimed at civilians and cannot be separated from terrorism against Israel. Osama Bin-Laden himself linked the two, so far be it for me to separate the two.

Maher Bitar summed up the fact that his calls for boycotting Israel are incitement to destroy Israel when he said, "I have not personally suffered any racism, but it's about the system." After all his claims about how Israelis mistreat Muslims, Bitar could not honestly claim that he was a victim of what he had previously claimed he was a victim of all during the conference. So much for him as being the expert presenter he claimed to be. I may have been the only person in the room who picked up on the key phrase referring to Israel "it's about the system," the classic phrase revolutionaries have used in calling for the overthrow of governments. I do not believe those words were an accident. Here Bitar stated he wants to get rid of the system in Israel, meaning Jews governing Jews.

One of my absolute favorite quotes that day was when Nadeem Muaddi said: "Without divestment, boycott and sanctions, we would be living in Bantustans." This was the wording of Professor Boyle, thus indicating again that Boyle had a direct involvement in the conference. Incidentally, prior to my arrival at Georgetown, I had emailed one of the organizers requesting an interview with Boyle at Georgetown. I was told Boyle was "not able to attend." The response was very similar to the one I received at Ohio State, further indicating the event organizers knew exactly who he is and just as with Ohio State, they would have liked for him to attend.

Soon after that session ended, I walked through a row of vendor tables where people could buy communist revolution books, AK 47 rifle pins, and other propaganda. I do not think it was a coincidence that many of the items offered for sale are also for sale on neo-Nazi websites, and at better prices than I what I had seen at Georgetown. Then the word leaked out, and there was a which-hunt to exclude Jews from the conference despite it being in full swing. People like Rachel Fish from the David Project were suddenly excluded from attending events. When sitting with her at a far back table, Rachel warned me, "You had better not sit with me or they will know who you are and lock you out too." I stood up and left Rachel, who was obviously sad and upset. As an observant Jew, she had nowhere to go since it was the Jewish Sabbath, so she sat alone to make sure nobody else she knew would be ejected. Rachel was looking out for my best interests, which I appreciated. Still, I felt bad for her.

I had only known Rachel by reputation prior to the Georgetown hate-fest and may have spoken to her on the phone only once. Rachel is the activist's activist and an overall kind and brilliant woman. I found it rather amusing that I was not exposed in that Zionist witch-hunt, but I had caught the attention of the Georgetown University administration. They assigned a university official, and not a just conference student, to chase after and escort me as I was taking a walk toward the cafeteria building to see the event postings of the various campus organizations, so I told my inquisitor I was headed for a cup of coffee. I realized I was under suspicion, especially after my comment challenging the photograph, but they were clearly unable to make a photo match of me. At that point I became unsure of who was conducting the witch hunt to evict Zionists attending, the event organizers, the university or both.

Since I had never had an escort before, I decided to have fun with it, especially since nobody else was afforded the privilege of having a university vice-president with them. Georgetown is a private university and I was its guest, but I hardly think other university guests received such wonderful treatment. I engaged my watchdog in a conversation where it became obvious neither of us trusted each other, as we spoke about the most obscure topics that came to our minds. I brushed off his questions about the publication I worked for and quickly turned the topic to Georgetown University and its escort policy, thanking them glowingly all the while. I then made my personal proctor wait outside a bathroom for more than twenty minutes only because I could. I confused him more when I told him I changed my mind about the coffee. Little did he realize I had no money in my pocket at the time since it was the Jewish Sabbath. Despite this, I managed to maintain my cover with a university official who probably feared bad public relations from my report.

Sunday morning proved most interesting. I sat in the back at the closing press conference, alone, when someone suddenly sat next to me and began asking a bunch of questions about the magazine where I claimed to work. The only thing I could think of was that my cover was blown while I was desperately trying to take notes. I was just waiting to be thrown out when the person who identified himself as Eric whispered suddenly, "I'm a Zionist." I then realized who he probably was, but I didn't want to blow my cover in case my hunch was wrong.

While sitting with Eric, I was watching a closing panel discussion with Noura Erakat listening to multiple shouts of "From the river to the sea!" from the audience with no challenges or decorum requests from the panel. This inaction indicated that they approved the audience's message for the complete destruction of Israel and replacing it with a Palestinian state. When I heard a rather inaudible short comment from a pro-Israel elderly man, Erakat immediately had him ejected. As he was beginning to stand, lifting himself up with his cane, I saw Georgetown University police officers grab the man forcefully and then physically drag the old man out of the hall with his cane in tow as he screamed in agony. At the time, I was certified as an Emergency Medical Technician, National Registry, so I immediately followed him out to make sure he was not injured. I later learned his name is Bill Maniaci, a veteran on the United States Army, and a lawsuit may have been filed on his behalf considering how Georgetown police officers had abused him.

After the closing press conference Sunday morning, there were some protests outside the main building. While speaking with some Jewish Georgetown students in the fenced-in, pro-Israel, protest area, Muaddi and Bitar were walking by us slowly, listening intently to what we were saying. At the moment they were just two feet away, Mikhail Alterman introduced me by name to a student. Muaddi and Bitar both suddenly stopped dead in their tracks, and Muaddi practically went into convulsions right then and there: they clearly knew my name and were upset. They suddenly found out I, as their number one foe, was at the Palestine Solidarity Movement hate-fest at Georgetown all along. My cover was blown, but at that point it didn't matter. The organizers were rather unhappy to know I had been right in front of them all along, especially at the Christian Outreach session.

They were fearful of me because they knew that I would surely expose their false photo and deplorable tactics. I just ignored them as they watched me having conversations with students and eventually walked away. A little while later, I went to talk to the university official who had earlier escorted me to get a cup of coffee. By this point he clearly knew exactly who I am and was rather unamused, to put it mildly. The rage on his face was unmistakable now that he knew my identity. We were all leaving, so having me thrown out was a moot point. Mikhail and I were followed to the gate on our way out, so I decided to milk our escort's time a little more as we spoke about where we would eat lunch. The feelings were mutual when we finally left the campus—we did not want to stay and the university was clearly happy we finally left.

For hosting the conference, Georgetown University reportedly received tens of millions of dollars from the Saudi Royal Family for an endowment fund to pay for a Chair in Arab Studies in the Georgetown University Center for Contemporary Arab Studies. A document about the center published on the Georgetown University website entitled, "Center for Contemporary Arab Studies History," states the following:

> Students, faculty, and the community have the opportunity to learn from an impressive and varied list of invited speakers who provide an academic context for understanding the Arab region. The public affairs program now stands as an essential part of the Center and the student experience, hosting or sponsoring over 75 events each year. These events provide a forum for academics, policy makers, representatives from nongovernmental organizations, political leaders, activists, filmmakers, visual artists, authors, and musicians from the Arab world, the United States, and other countries.
>
> The Center's annual two-day symposium has attracted scholars from all over the world. The Center continues to attract expert faculty who publish widely and serve as a resource to the media, such as the Washington Post, NPR, CNN, and Al-Jazeera. Besides teaching, these professors travel internationally, engaging in research projects and joint conferences, and bring dynamic learning back to Georgetown. They play an active role in professional associations, such as the Middle East Studies Association.
>
> Dissemination of information and analyses beyond the campus is a priority. Through its publications and website, the Center is well known within the academic and greater community. Publications include occasional papers, books,

and online articles. The Center's newsletter now reaches over
4,500 local, national, and overseas readers.

In this statement, Georgetown University says they are encouraging Arab
activism by specifically listing activism as an essential part of their media
information campaign. Although I have been a guest on both networks, I
thought it was very interesting that the Georgetown statement mentioned Al-
Jazeera Television, but not Fox News.

Georgetown University does not present Israel's side on the Middle-East
conflict, which is diametrically opposed to what is stated in its own mission
statement that school was supposedly built on: "...principles in the diversity
of our students, faculty, and staff, our commitment to justice and the common
good, our intellectual openness, and our international character." This bias
should not be surprising.

While Georgetown may have been the perfect venue for the Palestinian
Solidarity Movement conference, the question still remains why hate-fest
organizers target Christians and churches. The answer to this is the growing alliance of Christians and Jews in support of Israel, as led by Christians
United for Israel.[2] This alliance is the exact opposite of a boycott. The bringing
together of Christians and Jews sitting down together for a proverbial cup of
coffee is the exact opposite of the division and divisive message central to the
Arab boycott of Israel. Alliances bring people together by definition, while the
Arab world wants to separate people as demonstrated by Arab League's plan to
isolate Jews from the rest of the world. The Arab plan was defined by Palestine
Liberation Organization and Palestinian Authority consultant Francis Boyle.
To accomplish their mission, Muslin students have told Christians to lie to
clergy and congregants in their houses of worship, and to purposely deceive
their clergy who are working in the name of their God, all in the name of Islam.
That was the "Arab moderate" view of how to create peace.

After I returned home from that hate-fest, I wrote a letter to Georgetown
University President John J. DeGioia about the incitement to violence I had
witnessed, telling him that if I hear of anyone being injured as a result of
actions taken from the hate-fest, I would gladly assist in any lawsuit against

2.www.cufi.org

the university. In addition to spending about $60,000 for added security over a single weekend, Georgetown University has built a prejudicial educational department and student base, thanks to imparting hate in generations to come. Although the hate-fest generated negative publicity and lost alumni donations, the message from the Arab world is clear—hosting Israel hate-fests may give you a black eye, but the university will make millions of dollars in the process. In other words, thanks to the help of the Arab world, promoting hatred of Israel and Jews is profitable.

Pittsburgh

At the University of Pittsburgh, the Pittsburgh Palestine Solidarity Committee held its "Divest from Israeli Apartheid" weekend October 23-25, 2009. I have a few things to say about this. First, the name is a complete misnomer. As previously proved, Israel is a pluralistic society, whereas Palestinian Arabs actually practice apartheid by completely banning Jews from their areas. The agenda for the conference, which was also titled the "Boycott, Divestment Sanctions Conference, University of Pittsburgh," included the following workshops:

1. BDS Skill-Building Workshops. The conference began with a workshop giving students specific information on how to illegally further the Arab boycott of Israel. This event set the tone for the entire weekend by getting students fired up to destroy Israel economically and divide nations, rather than seeking peace.

2. How to Research Corporations Involved in Israeli Occupation and Apartheid. In addition to boycotting Israel themselves, students were instructed on how to form witch-hunts to see who is working with Jews. This session was designed to place blame on every company with business dealings with Israel, as the session's specific goal was to economically isolate any and every company that even thinks about doing business with Israel. Not only is this in direct violation of U.S. Antiboycott

laws for supplying information to further the Arab boycott, but it is also designed to indoctrinate an entire generation to intimidate their future coworkers into not conducting any business with Israel.

3. How to Research Your University's Investments. This seminar encouraged academic boycotts, the modern equivalent of book burnings, by telling universities not to cooperate with Israeli universities in research. In fact, the seminar encouraged the audience to not even allow books by Israeli authors, especially those in academia. The students were told to become thought police and thus deny all kinds of literature and publications by Jewish authors. This session advocated the formation of another Kristallnacht!

4. Creative Arts in Activism: English translation—graffiti. Here, they essentially advocated vandalism and the defacing of public property.

5. Academic and Cultural Boycotts: Israel's culture is the Jewish culture. Dr. Martin Luther King, Jr.'s statement, "When people criticize Zionists, they mean Jews. You're talking anti-Semitism!" is directly applied here. This is a boycott of the Jewish religion and Jewish education, further demonstrating the Arab boycott was designed to separate people and not bring them together for peace.

The Pittsburgh conference ended with what they called a "Theatrical production of My Name is Rachel Corrie." Of course this is a fantasized story of how the "Evil Israeli Army" murdered the poor girl. I say, "Evil Israeli Army" for a reason—those are their words. The organizers overtly blamed a faceless entity that cannot speak for itself, yet this term is what every Palestinian calls every Israeli to justify his indiscriminate murder of Israelis. This conference, too, claimed that since all Israelis are inherently part of the IDF as reservists, all Israelis are inherently legitimate targets for terrorism. In their own words, the Palestinians partake in a "legitimate armed struggle" and therefore all Israelis are legitimate targets.

From beginning to end, the University of Pittsburgh, Pennsylvania Boycott, Divestment, Sanctions event was meant to indoctrinate students to hate Jews, not just Israel, and taxpayer dollars actually paid for a portion of it. It was filled with lies, starting with the first session where Arabs misdirected shame for their own apartheid policies on Israel. The lies continued to the end where the Arabs blamed Israel for their own murder of Rachel Corrie. The Palestinians kept claiming they were the victims of "Israeli aggression" while never owning up to their promoting terrorism. In fact, the promotional materials for the group included incitement to violence with photos glorifying the throwing of rocks at civilians to physically harm people. This is all in the name of what the Palestinian activists consider peace, yet it is in reality a call for the incitement of violence.

Across The Nation

If you think these are isolated incidents, you are wrong. Single events and entire weekends like this occur across the nation on a regular basis, and this with the direct knowledge of university officials, who otherwise preach tolerance on their campuses. The campus groups sponsoring the events do so as student government-commissioned, campus organizations at state universities or private schools, and they receive government funding in the former. Letters to the presidents of universities in these matters are largely ignored.

I have worked with two Jewish students at Case Western Reserve University in Cleveland, Ohio, who have left that school due to what they said were too many anti-Semitic events, including several anti-Israel speakers brought to the campus by anti-Semitic tenured faculty. CWRU reportedly offered some balance, but I ask what balance is there to hate? Are they suggesting it is proper to have the Ku Klux Klan speak on a campus as long as there is a counter-program, and if so why are the Jewish students the ones who have to organize and pay for events countering the hate events paid for with the deep pockets of a university? Is that what universities such as CWRU consider balance?

Susan Tuchman, the legal director at the Zionist Organization of America, has filed civil rights discrimination cases against California universities on

behalf of students. Meanwhile, the Westboro Baptist Church protested the Hillel at the University of Oklahoma for conducting Rosh Hashanna/Jewish New
Year services in 2009. Yes, the Westboro Baptist Church is known for outra-
geous protests, but it both illustrates the underlying level of hatred that Jews
face on campuses and how little people care, since that was not a top news
story.

Jewish students are all too often under constant attack just for being Jewish, yet this prejudice is excused as being just anti-Israel or just anti-Zionist.
This is nothing more than a poor excuse. Some Jews think it is, for a lack
of better words, the normal day to day anti-Semitism they experience, but it
is not. Anti-Semitism, which has long been simmering quietly on campuses,
has resurfaced because people are accepting what Dr. Martin Luther King, Jr.
warned against when he said, "Don't talk like that! When people criticize
Zionists, they mean Jews. You're talking anti-Semitism!" Meanwhile, to Jews
on some campuses, hate has become a regular occurrence. Here is the alarm
bell—RING! I hope you heard it.

From Boycott to Goldstone

CHAPTER 13

There is no better way to say it: boycotts do not bring peace. If I were at a protest, I would say, "No Commerce, No Peace," because you cannot have peace with someone you will not sit down with for a cup of coffee. You will sit with a friend for a cup of coffee, but not with an enemy. If you want to be friends with someone, a cup of coffee is a good place to start; however, becoming friends is not something that happens overnight. You also cannot sign a piece of paper to become instant friends, which is why peace treaties for the sake of peace never work. Peace builds with time, when all parties truly want to see it flourish, and a quick glance at the history of the world proves it. Let's examine the lessons from history.

The United States and Canada were not always at peace. The War of 1812 included the invasion of Canada, but over time trade built peace between the two nations. The United States and Canada now share the world's largest unmonitored border for a reason—the two nations rely on each other economically, which is why the peace between the United States and Canada is so strong that it cannot be dissolved easily. The two former warring nations simply cannot afford to break the peace and will therefore work out all differences no matter what. The United States and the British fought both in the American Revolution and the War of 1812, after which peace was built on trade based on the demand for common goods.

Just the same, when the United States and France had a dispute over Iraq, the economic reliance between the United States and France was so strong that the damaging of relations was not in either nation's best interest. U.S. consumers, however, reacted by starting a boycott of French products that spawned a French counter-boycott of U.S. products. In the fervor, some people started using the silly term "Freedom Fries," but that was not something which affected trade, since Americans were frying American potatoes all along. During this time, I was the leading monitor of the U.S. boycott of French products and associated boycotting websites; thus, I can say with authority that this was an effective, albeit short-term, boycott. Other than a few people in Congress, the leaders of both countries remained silent on the issue because they knew consumer anger would eventually subside; besides, they had little interest perpetuating that boycott. Even at the peak of that boycott, the U.S. military used French-made Zodiac inflatable boats.

When speaking about the U.S. in Iraq, President George H.W. Bush said that democracy brings peace between nations. He was wrong. Trade brings peace. The U.S.S.R. and Cuba have peace based on trade, not democracy. The United States and Cuba, on the other hand, have no trade and no peace. While Israel and Egypt technically have peace due to a treaty, it is a cold peace because the trade between those two nations is virtually nonexistent. The only real trade in the Middle East between Israel and an Arab nation is with Jordan, and that trade is growing along with peace because those two nations are slowly becoming more economically reliant on each other. As for the democracy claim, Israel is a democracy, while Jordan is a dictatorship, thus disproving President Bush's assertion. Israel and Jordan are literally and proverbially sitting down together for coffee; that is how peace thrives!

In becoming trading partners, an inherent understanding is built between people. This happened in the United States during the Civil Rights Movement. By banning segregated seating, for example, people had to sit next to each other in restaurants. Of course there was much more to it than just that, but getting people to sit down together is the first step. The Arab boycott of Israel is designed for one purpose—to destroy Israel—and the separation of people through the boycott is the fundamental methodology of the Arab world. They want to economically isolate Israel to destroy its economy. Boycotts are the antithesis of peacemaking.

The Arab world knows this, which is why they push their boycott. While claiming to negotiate for peace in good faith at the Wye River Accords, Yasser Arafat was also pushing to expand the Arab boycott in Malaysia. This proved Arafat and the Palestinian Authority, along with Boyle and his negotiating team, had intentions other than peace all along. The Arab boycott of Israel is economic warfare used to perpetuate strife.

The boycott of Jewish interests, as it was called when first declared, resulted in the creation of the unifying body to coordinate the boycott—the Arab League. It is the same Arab League that both created the Central Boycott Office, which coordinates the Israel boycott efforts of every member state, and has voted for unified military action against Israel. The Arab boycott was officially declared in 1921, which is 27 years before Israel was established as an independent state. Just like putting out a fire, you must tackle the root source of the fire and not simply just blow smoke away so the sky looks good. If you truly want peace in the Middle East, the Arab boycott must end!

The Palestinian Authority is the Palestine Liberation Organization

The advent of the Oslo Accords put the duty of prevention of war with Israel, including terrorism, away from the Arab nations and into the hands of the Palestine Liberation Organization/Palestinian Authority and its Fateh terrorist subsidiary. After all, proxy fights give Arab states plausible denial. While people see right through the thin veil of disguise that Iran uses when it controls and funds Hezbollah in Lebanon, the Arab world and Iran enjoy the diplomatic cover. The same applies to Saudi Arabia, which claims to be a moderate nation, despite paying stipends to the families of suicide bombers and thus encourages such terrorist activity. The PLO/PA has become a tool to coordinate the overall Arab campaign.

If you think the PLO is defunct, you are seriously mistaken. According to the United States government's Foreign Agent Registration Act website, FARA, the Palestine Liberation Organization is the active entity that files current reports about its activities under the FARA law. The Palestine Liberation Organization, which is recognized as a terrorist organization, is still the entity that the United States recognized as representing the Arabs against Israel. Semantics aside, nothing has changed.

In fact, the website of the official Palestinian representation to the United States government, http://www.plomission.us, calls itself the PLO Mission to the United States. As stated on the website, "Welcome: Palestine Liberation Organization (PLO) website—The Official Voice of Palestine in the U.S."

> The Palestine Liberation Organization Mission in Washington, DC is the official representative of the PLO in the United States. Its primary objective is to protect and promote the interests of the Palestinian people in the United States, through official relations with the U.S. government, commercial contacts with the business community, and through public outreach and educational efforts aimed at fostering a better understanding of Palestine and Palestinians amongst the American public at large.

Let's start by lifting the veil. They call themselves the Palestine Liberation Organization, and so should we. They have obviously rejected both the politically correct name Palestinian Authority, which had given them a clean slate, and their separation from the terrorism associated with the name. They have had years to change their name to what the Clinton Administration granted them through the Oslo Accords, and their lack of action tells me they do not want the new name. They are the PLO, and they want to be known as the PLO; therefore, there is no reason anyone should call them anything else.

Their website is full of historical inaccuracies, including the claim that all of Israel is historic Palestine, despite there never actually being a state of Palestine. The Palestine region of the Ottoman Empire did at one time include all of what is now Jordan; however, the PLO fails to mention Jordan was cut out of what was meant to be Israel in order to form an Arab-Palestinian state as the final border. There is a reason for that—the PLO was established in 1964, a full 16 years after Israel had become an independent nation, in order to coordinate terrorist groups. The PLO was formed to annihilate Israel and nothing has changed since.

The word commerce in the PLO description refers to commerce with businesses that boycott Israel. Since the PLO Mission has diplomatic immunity, it does not have to worry about the illegalities of the boycott within the U.S. despite the U.S. Antiboycott laws. Besides, it has people like Boyle who strategize with it and encourage student groups to spread such venom. The official PLO website encourages these efforts with links to sites such as the Electronic Intifada that states, "All EI founders and team members are opposed to all forms of violence against civilians by any actor in the conflict." However, this group does not consider Israelis to be civilians since they all serve in the IDF reserves, which is their semantics game.

A primary mission of the Electronic Intifada organization is to promote the Arab boycott, which is on their website at http://electronicintifada.net/bytopic/boycott-divestment-sanctions.shtml. The PLO publicly endorses the boycott since it a primary function of the Electronic Intifada, a boycott which includes, according to the EI website, "Academic boycott(s), consumer boycott(s), cultural boycott(s), church divestment(s), and university divestment." The group also includes the wording "other divestment," which they describe as the following: "Divestment is not an option limited to churches and universities. States, cities, unions and banks are also being called on to withdraw their investments from Israel Bonds and corporations and institutions that play a role in the occupation." In other words, the EI calls for the complete boycott of Israel.

Exposing Silent Support of the PLO

The PLO attitude that all of Israel is Palestine is not just held among some radical students or the PLO leadership; rather, it is the mainstream ideology of Arabs and Israel-haters that is often not voiced due to its politically incorrect nature. When Arabs and their supporters speak of Palestine and ignore Israel, it is code for Palestine to completely replace Israel. They just leave that inconvenient point out of the conversation in order to keep people focused on their hateful messages. One of the most prominent so-called Lebanese-Americans accidentally proved this point, someone who had a reputation of being anti-Israel in her reporting, someone who even went as far as to mask her heritage. Eventually, however, her true feelings came out and were videotaped for the world to see.

Helen Thomas was born August 4, 1920, in Winchester, Kentucky. It is interesting that she claims to be Lebanese, since her father is Syrian, which comports with the Syrian political stance that Lebanon is really Southern Syria, thereby justifying its occupation and control of Lebanon[1]. The fact that Helen considers herself to be Lebanese is probably so that she can appear more acceptable to the American public due to the historically strained U.S and Syrian relations. According to the U.S. State Department, "Syria has been on the U.S. list of state sponsors of terrorism since the list's inception in 1979." Although the U.S. maintains an embassy in Syria, the U.S. recalled its ambassador in 1986.

In discussing the status of U.S. and Syrian relations, the State Department revealed how "safe" it is for Americans to be in Syria:

> On September 12, 2006, the U.S. Embassy was attacked by four armed assailants with guns, grenades, and a car bomb (which failed to detonate). Syrian security forces successfully countered the attack, killing all four attackers. Two other Syrians killed during the attack were a government security guard

---

1.http://www.nndb.com/people/857/000022791/

and a passerby. The Syrian Government publicly stated that terrorists had carried out the attack. The U.S. Government has not received an official Syrian Government assessment of the motives or organization behind the attack, but security was upgraded at U.S. facilities. Both the Syrian ambassador to the U.S., Imad Moustapha, and President Bashar Asad, however, blamed U.S. foreign policy in the region for contributing to the incident.[2]

Syria is a brutal dictatorship and nothing happens there without government approval. The fact that Syria blames the U.S. for its attack on the U.S. embassy is not only absurd, but it demonstrates why Helen prefers to be thought of as Lebanese and not Syrian.

The U.S. State Department also states the following on its website:

> While most Syrians appear genuinely friendly towards foreigners, underlying tensions can lead to a quick escalation in the potential for violence. In a few recent examples: an American reported being verbally harassed and told 'you Americans are not welcome here' after he avoided stepping on an Israeli flag that had been placed on the ground in a shopping area. In another incident, an American riding in a taxi, sensing anti-American sentiment from the driver, said they were from another country. Upon hearing this, the driver told them 'Good, because if you were American I would kill you.' On another occasion, an American reported that a Syrian military vehicle pulled up next to him and mimicked actions of running him off the road.[3]

Let's face it. Americans neither place Syria high on their must-see travel list nor trust Syrians, and with incidents like these, is it really all that surprising?

Helen has been a member of the White House Press Corps since J.F.K. was President in 1961, and is famous for her tough questions. In respect for her

2.http://www.state.gov/r/pa/ei/bgn/3580.htm
3.http://travel.state.gov/travel/cis_pa_tw/cis/cis_1035.html

longevity, she has been given the first question in every press conference since Ronald Reagan's presidency, and she has sat in the center seat in the front row of the White House Press Briefing Room for many years. However, her career ended abruptly after her true nature was revealed.

On Thursday, May 27, 2010, Rabbi David F. Nesenoff, the founder of RabbiLIVE.com[4], attended the White House Jewish Heritage Celebration with several others. On his way out, the group came across Helen on the front lawn of the White House. In a later appearance on the Fox News Channel, Rabbi Nesenoff said he thought the chance meeting with the prestigious and famous journalist would be a great learning opportunity for his son. He was correct. With a video camera in hand, Rabbi Nesenoff asked Helen about the state of journalism, for which received a coherent response. When he next asked her for advice on Israel, Helen responded with a shocking and anti-Semitic tirade: "Tell them to get the hell out of Palestine... go home (to) Poland, Germany."

On Thursday, June 3, 2010, Rabbi Nesenoff posted the video of the conversation on his website. The video was so shocking that it was rapidly shared on the Internet, garnering 1.5 Million views in just a few days. It instantly became the most blogged and talked about viral video in Jewish and political circles.

Her specific statements regarding Poland and Germany can easily be interpreted as meaning Israelis should return to the Nazi concentration camps. She only added the U.S. to her list of countries Jews should return to soften her remarks. Regardless of how you interpret her first mentioning Poland and Germany, the statement is akin to telling African-Americans to go back to Africa or telling Asian-Americans to return to Asia. Her statement was bigoted, racist and anti-Semitic any which way you look at it. The fact that it came from a prestigious White House correspondent made it all the more shocking. Nobody imagined those words would come from someone who has a reserved seat mere inches from and unprecedented access to every United States president the last 50 years.

As the news of the video spread, a wildfire started where many groups called for her to be fired and banned from the White House Press Corps. In fact, people began questioning if other journalists would or should attend

---

4.http://www.rabbilive.com

White House briefings with her in the room. People from all sides of the political spectrum excoriated Helen, including President Obama's White House Press Secretary Robert Gibbs, and former Republican presidential candidate Mike Huckabee. I was shocked to see former Democrat presidential campaign manager and Fox News contributor Bob Beckel actually defend Helen on television during the height of the scandal.

June 6, 2010, was a pivotal Sunday. The political pressure was mounting and the end of her journalism career became apparent when her agent for speaking engagements dropped Helen. We have seen this before with other celebrities as nobody wants to be seen as the last person associated with a fallen celebrity—remember Dan Rather?

The next day, Helen's employer, Hearst Corporation, issued the following press release:

HELEN THOMAS ANNOUNCES RETIREMENT
WASHINGTON, June 7, 2010—Helen Thomas announced Monday that she is retiring, effective immediately.

Her decision came after her controversial comments about Israel and the Palestinians were captured on videotape and widely disseminated on the Internet.

Thomas later issued a statement: "I deeply regret my comments I made last week regarding the Israelis and the Palestinians. They do not reflect my heart-felt belief that peace will come to the Middle East only when all parties recognize the need for mutual respect and tolerance. May that day come soon."

Thomas will mark her 90th birthday on August 4.

The timing of the press release, a Monday morning, and the fact that Helen was not at the morning press briefing clearly indicates there were serious conversations over the weekend regarding her employment status. The announcement of her immediate retirement coupled with a halfhearted apology tells me she was fired. In her apology, Helen failed to address both her blatant anti-Semitism and calls to abolish Israel when she said Jews should "get the hell out of Palestine." Her comment demonstrated the stance of the Palestine Liberation Organization, which demonstrates the desire for the complete destruction of Israel as seen in its logo of all of Israel as being the Palestinian state.

Helen was not just echoing her own radical position that Jews should get out of the Middle East and Israel be destroyed; rather, she espoused the Hamas, Hezbollah and Palestine Liberation Organization stance of driving the Jews into the sea. The goal of eliminating all Jews from Israel is part of the Arab war strategy. Where war has not worked, terrorist strikes target Israelis, Jews and any other Israel supporters. For those who cannot engage in terrorism, boycott campaigns are promoted. People who wish to destroy Israel will neither show any friendship toward Israel nor buy any Israeli products because that is their economic vehicle to destroy Israel.

These are the mainstream views of Arabs and their supporters. They just don't want to repeat Helen's words because they don't want to be seen as the hate mongers they really are. As evidenced by the video, Helen was not alone when revealing the extent of her hatred, as her assistants neither said anything to mitigate her comments nor apologized on her behalf. Rabbi Nesenoff had his video camera in hand and was not hiding it. Helen Thomas did not have any reason to think she was speaking in private, yet still managed to reveal her true nature, the sentiments of the pro-Palestine movement, and her agreement with the views of the Palestine Liberation Organization.

When you hear people say Palestine when speaking about Israel, they are revealing their true nature in a poor attempt to be politically correct. They are soft-balling their argument for the listener who does not know their code words, but now you do.

The PLO Rule

The only exceptions to direct PLO rule is Hamas, in Gaza, which acts as a separate government and attacks Israel from the south; and Hezbollah in Lebanon, which Iran both finances and arms in order to attack Israel from the north. Regardless, both listen to the PLO leadership. While the PLO facilitates terrorism against Israel, its leaders do not want outside military attacks because that can potentially destabilize their own internal power and more importantly, harm their intentionally false-façade. The Palestinians are essentially playing a status quo game until the world forces a state upon them, so they have something to complain about. An imposed state will give the PLO an excuse to fight Israel further. If the PLO accepts final border status as part of a peace negotiation, it will have to accept Israel as a legitimate state, which it cannot do politically, lest their leadership risk being overthrown by its own people in a civil war. As we will soon see, the PLO has been playing this same blame game over Gaza since Israel's withdrawal.

Meanwhile, the power struggles between Arab heads of state is more important to some Arab leaders than their fight with Israel, a factor which has inadvertently protected Israel. The proof of this was the war between Iran and Iraq. Iran was only able to focus on Israel, once the United States took Saddam Hussein out of the picture. Israel was content to have both Iraq and Iran busy, but now that Iran has the time on its hands, it can focus on building weapons to destroy Israel, and perhaps other Western interests.

The main objective of the Arab world has been to destroy Israel, and only the methods have changed with time.

Goldstone

The United Nations Fact Finding Mission on the Gaza Conflict, more commonly known as the Goldstone Commission Report or just "Goldstone," did not happen in a vacuum. The Palestinian Authority had fully planned and promoted it as the next stage of its efforts to destroy Israel. The Arab world has been fighting with Jews and Israel for more than 100 years, first to prevent Israel from being formed and then later to destroy Israel. Every step of that plan has clearly failed, and the plans to destroy Israel have evolved with the Arabs always vilifying Jews, while masking their true intent. The Central Boycott Office in Damascus, Syria has always maintained a low profile outside the Arab world, and so have the official plans to expand the boycott. Unfortunately for the Arab world, I will now expose the truth about the Goldstone report; specifically, how it is directly associated with Boyle and the Arab boycott of Israel. Here are the facts:

The Arab-Israeli conflict started with strife and small boycotts, leading up to an organized, but failed, boycott in 1921. As we know, Israel was established as a state in 1948, and the Arab world was outraged. Arab leaders told their people to get out of the way temporarily so they could immediately destroy Israel, but the Arab nations not only failed to destroy Israel but also lost land to the Jews in the process, despite the barely existent Israeli army being poorly armed and marginally organized. The Arab nations' response was to blame others, including the United States, for their own failures. Soon after, the Central Boycott Office was established to coordinate all Arab League member boycotts and strengthen the overall Arab world resolve to boycott Israel. Because the war and boycotts failed, Muslims began using terrorist activities more often, including the hijacking of airplanes, murdering Olympic athletes, cross border raids to murder women and children, and rocket attacks. The Arab world continues to use every method it can to attack Jews. Where specific actions no longer work against Israel, those same methods, such as hijacking airplanes, are used in the rest of the world as evidenced by the World Trade Center attack on September 11, 2001.

Land for peace has also failed over and over again. This idea has failed primarily because trading land for peace had zero guarantees of peace, not to mention there is zero peace in return. The Arabs even proposed that Israel negotiate land for peace deals with every Arab nation, which would mean giving land to every Arab nation and effectively leaving Israel with practically nothing. Of course, Israel patently rejected this idea since it would mean that Arab armies would quickly invade and decimate Israel in no time at all. Israel will never accept such terms, despite the Arab world's irrational demands for it.

One person changed the dynamics in the past several years, one Francis A. Boyle, the earlier mentioned international law professor who teaches at the College of Law at the University of Illinois at Urbana-Champaign. Per his resume, which he posted on the Internet, Boyle's legal practice has included working for the PLO since 1987, but I have been unable to locate his name on filings on the Foreign Agent Registration Act website.

We have already discussed how Boyle stated he created the divest-from-Israel campaign, which he includes as one of great accomplishments in his resume. Yes, in his resume Boyle brags about how created a movement to thwart peace and promote terrorism. In fact, Boyle brags about how he made the war crimes claim against Israel, which bolsters Palestinian groups that possess maps as part of their logo showing all of Israel being Palestine. It is not just individual Palestinians or their supporters who use that logo. In fact, if you were to lookup "Palestine" at FARA.gov, the Foreign Agent Registration Act website, you will see that the Palestinian delegation not only uses a map of all of Israel in their logo, but it even calls itself the Palestine Liberation Organization. Once again, the PLO terrorist organization is registered and functions as the official arm of the Palestinians. They have not changed their name despite Israel haters claiming otherwise. The openly stated goal listed in their official filings may claim to be achieving peace in the Middle East, but they never say peace with Israel. In reality the PLO clearly demonstrates its continued goal since day one in seeking the destruction of Israel.

Boyle may act as if he is naive, but he is a consultant to the PLO, which openly calls for Israel's total destruction. He must have seen the map in the logo of the organization he works for which shows Palestine completely replacing Israel. Partly with my help in exposing the true aim of the divest-from-Israel campaign via my Divestment Watch website and articles, the divest-from-Israel campaign failed, which is why Boyle, a consultant to the PLO, derived his war crimes claim. Boyle was and has been working with the PLO when he created the war crimes claim as proven by his own resume. I can logically conclude that just like Boyle's other action plans to destroy Israel in conjunction and in consultation with the PLO, the war crimes claim was a plan he had hatched with the PLO. That makes the war crimes claim, along with the divest-from-Israel campaign, part of the official Arab boycott, and inherently the overall Arab plan to destroy Israel.

The first manifestation of the war crimes claim is when Israeli President Shimon Peres was accused of war crimes. These war crimes claims, of course, were primarily based on the false charge that Israel occupies Gaza, but that is not true since Israel left Gaza, which was autonomous at the time of the events of the charges. This is not say that Israel did nothing wrong; everyone makes some mistakes. Rather, I am just saying the very basis for the war crimes charge is false because none of Israel's actions in Gaza constituted war crimes. More to the point though, you cannot have an autonomous occupation; as previously stated, this is an oxymoron. Besides, can you name the nation that Gaza was contained in before Israel took control over it in war? The answer is none since there has never been a nation called Palestine and Egypt had never claimed it. It was a stateless territory; thus, there was no state for Israel to have occupied it from. Any way you look at it, there was never any occupation of Gaza by Israel because Gaza never filled the definition. When you hear the word "occupation," you must always ask, "Occupied from which country?" If you cannot answer the question, then you cannot fulfill the definition of occupation. The concept of Gaza occupation is a legal fallacy.

Despite this, there were threats that President Peres would be arrested and put on trial if he stepped foot in certain European counties, a threat that failed since Mr. Peres simply stayed in Israel. I am sure Boyle liked that, since it accomplished his goal of isolating Israel, in this case a key Israeli official, from the world community. Once again, the PLO stepped up their efforts in response, like always; this time they followed Boyle's plan and declared Israel as war criminals, meaning the entire state was guilty of war crimes. When that did not gain attention, Boyle decided to turn his efforts to getting the entire United Nations to accept his claim of Israel being a war crimes state as the first step of the process to have Israel removed from the United Nations, which in turn would de-legitimize the country. The fact that he worked to remove Israel from the United Nations is clear proof that his goal is the total destruction of Israel. This is where the Goldstone commission becomes the center of the PLO plan to destroy Israel.

In his article titled "Law and Disorder in the Middle East," Boyle said that Israel "must be suspended on a *de facto* basis from any participation throughout the entire United Nations system." If that happens, an all-out-war to destroy Israel would occur, resulting in the genocide of Israeli men, women and children. Even the elderly would be considered legitimate targets by the Arab world since Israel would not be recognized as a legitimate nation. The complete destruction of Israel has been the goal of the Arab boycott from day one and as we see here, the PLO tried a modified plan after other methods had failed. One only has to look at the war crimes charge itself to disprove it. The charge is against Israel, not against individuals. This is in line with the PLO claim that since Israel requires all its citizens to serve in the army, then all Israelis are soldiers, combatants, and subject to indiscriminate terrorist attacks.

This was not a quickly conceived and executed plan. Boyle published his "Law and Disorder in the Middle East" in January, 2002. His plan had no teeth, so Arafat put it on the shelf; however, it was still worked on as part of Boyle's legal practice with the PLO as his client. After Arafat's death in 2004, Boyle pushed his ideas to his academic and international law colleagues, and his professional circle, and on January 11, 2009, a letter appeared in the London Times Online entitled "Israel's bombardment of Gaza is not self-defense—it's a war crime." The letter was from academics and lawyers, and it discussed Boyle's war crimes charges. Amongst the signers were Professor John B. Quigley of Ohio State University, which had hosted the divest-from-Israel hate-fest that included the presentation of the anti-Semitic video rant by Stokely Carmichael, and Professor Christine Chinkin of the London School of Economics who, just like Boyle, is a professor of International law. Is this a coincidence? Hardly. In fact, many criticized Chinkin for being a member of the United Nation's Goldstone Commission, due to the letter indicating she had already made up her mind prior to the investigation. Despite that letter being well known, she was never disqualified from being on that commission even though the letter clearly showed prejudice. This is evidence the commission was not only biased, but had a connection to the Boyle plan and the PLO.

Chinkin's participation in that commission was not an accident. The reason Chinkin was not removed from the Boyle Commission, I mean the Goldstone Commission, was that the entire United Nations Fact Finding Mission on the Gaza Conflict was based on Boyle's work, specifically Boyle's charges that he made in a speech to the United Nations, calling for Israel's destruction. The fact is that the United Nations Fact Finding Mission on the Gaza Conflict was a carefully orchestrated plan sanctioned by Boyle's employer, the Palestine Liberation Organization. Boyle does not act alone as an activist. His own articles brag about how he works with the PLO, how they "request" his help, and how Arafat did not always take his advice. Clearly, Boyle pressed the PLO further than they wanted to go at times, yet sooner or later they always adopted Boyle's advice.

The U.S. Congress rejected the adoption of the Goldstone Commission report findings due to the obviously ridiculous claims, but that does not mean the end of it. It still stands in high esteem in the United Nations; thus other nations may adopt it and press for various punitive punishments within the United Nations. We will likely see various adaptations of the Goldstone report in the near future. It has essentially become the new punching bag issue in the United Nations, that replaced the now-repealed "Zionism equals Racism" resolution, all thanks to Boyle.

The Parallel Campaign

The Palestinians had failed to destroy Israel so many times that they did not want to sit back and put all their proverbial eggs in one basket again; hence, they worked on a parallel track beginning with the Saudi Arabia plan. As much as the Palestinians need Boyle's help, they still do not completely trust him, as is seen with Arafat rejecting Boyle's rejection of the Olso treaty, which created a parallel campaign track. This distrust is also seen by the rejection of Boyle's War Crimes complaint, which followed that parallel tract with the 2002 Saudi Arabian plan just after they rejected Boyle's January, 2002 war crimes article. The Saudi plan to bypass Oslo and create a Palestinian state alongside Israel with the 1967 "Auschwitz" borders was categorically rejected by Israel. The Arabs recognize the failures of the Oslo agreements they signed; thus, they are trying to bypass it with the war crimes track. In the mean time, the Arabs still use the Oslo agreements, because it gives them some semblance of legitimacy.

Just as the Arabs later realized Boyle's rejection of Oslo would have been in their best interests, the Arab world now embraces Boyle's original war crimes concept. This is why there was a sudden push for that claim, culminating in the British academic letter signed by Chinkin and the push for the United Nations Fact Finding Mission on the Gaza Conflict, which was specifically designed to push the war crimes claim against Israel.

The Palestinians shelved Boyle's war crimes complaint until it was used with the United Nations Fact Finding Mission on the Gaza Conflict. The problem is, however, by the time Boyle's plan was put in action, Israel had already pulled out of Gaza in 2005, and that was from the small enclave of Jewish areas. The rest of Gaza was already under autonomous Palestinian control. Once Israel was completely out of all of Gaza, the Boyle plan had lost all of its teeth, so it again had to be modified. If it were not for the Goldstone commission, the Boyle complaints about Gaza would have gone to waste. The Goldstone commission would have also not been possible without the Boyle plan. Israel's withdrawal from Gaza left the Palestinians in a political public relations quandary, yet the Palestinians found a way to use it because that was all they had available if they were to compose new political attacks against Israel. The Palestinians got what they wanted. Jews leaving Gaza, however, was not good enough in their eyes, especially since Israel's pullout created a complaint vacuum; they could no longer blame Israel for everything in and about Gaza.

Once again, Palestinian plans to destroy Israel alternate between war, political attacks, boycotts and terrorism, yet they always return to the original base plan of the Arab League and their meetings to promote the Arab boycott of Israel. The war crimes claim is being spread by the divest-from-Israel crowd to recruit Americans under false pretenses, because there is no occupation to make the claim valid, but they don't tell people that. They also don't tell Americans the PLO had a direct role in creating the false claim. That is like deliberately painting a house neon pink, then complaining about the contractor for doing it. The Goldstone fraud is now exposed.

The Palestinian Game Plan

CHAPTER 14

Just as in sports, knowing the game plan of the other team gives one an advantage, and the same applies here. This book has exposed the working plans and methodologies of the Palestinians, including the truth behind the greater Arab League boycott of Israel. As we have seen, they are continually updating their plan. The following are their current and newest tactics that I see on the horizon, but you can always expect something new, especially since I have exposed the way they lie to people to recruit them for their libelous campaign to vilify Jews and destroy Israel. I call their methods libelous because I believe the Palestinians are knowingly making a false case and are purposely recruiting people to their campaign under false pretenses.

The Overall Plan

Goldstone failed when the U.S. House of Representatives overwhelmingly rejected the Goldstone report in November, 2009, which is why it virtually dropped off the news in the U.S. The Goldstone Commission was partly designed to sabotage the United States support for Israel because without political support from the United States, Israel would be an instant easy and open target for Arab countries to de-list as a legitimate nation. The defeat of Goldstone in the United States was a punch in the face to Boyle and his war crimes campaign, but Israel still faces many challenges.

In December, 2009, a British court issued an arrest warrant for Israeli Knesset Member Tzipi Livni, who had served as the Foreign Minister for Prime Minister Ehud Olmert during Israel's raid into Gaza to stop terrorist attacks. This was a move right out of Boyle's playbook: target modification, stealth attack, and then a new campaign to launch. It's another three-phase plan, which has Boyle's fingerprint all over it.

This is the signature of every Palestinian political attack plan. They are used to failure and keep trying new plans as soon as they drop the failed ones. From the Munich Olympics Massacre, to hijacking El-Al planes, to cross border terrorism, to failed Arab boycott attempts, the Palestinians keep trying new things within their playbook while always keeping the Arab boycott and terrorism as their base mission. Let's never forget that the terrorist attacks on September 11, 2001 were related to the United States supporting Israel. To Islamists, the United States is the "Big Satan" and Israel is the "Little Satan;" as much as they hate Israel, they loathe the United States even more.

The Palestinians are used to defeat, which is why they change their game plan so often. In their new plans, they are calling for a boycott of Israel as if such a boycott had never existed before. The idea is to both draw attention away from previous campaigns and to give potential recruits something 'new' on which to latch. What they don't want you to know, however, is that the renewed boycott calls are a complete diversion so people can complain that the boycott is nothing new. Their claim to launch a new boycott is a smoke and mirrors diversion from their real strategic campaign that began about thirty years before Israel was established and has been modified along the way to fit the realities of the day.

When the campus campaign to gain acceptance of the idea of a Palestinian state was in full speed in the 1980s, the idea was to build a future generation that would, once they had political and economic clout, be able to drive their campaign for the campaign's supporters. The Palestinians did not completely win that campaign, but did make some headway. As they continue the campus campaigns, the adults who were the campus targets thirty years ago are now being called to action to support the creation of a Palestinian state which will be used, as stated in their three phase plan, as the launching ground to destroy the rest of Israel. Peace cannot exist as long as that is the Palestinian plan, which is why ending the Arab boycott is the key to peace. Peace between Israel and its Arab neighbors can only thrive once the cost of war exceeds the economic loss of a broken peace. Trade is a barrier to war.

The campus campaign started about ten years ago as divestment from Israel then shifted to what they call "DBS," or Divestment, Boycott Sanctions. Later, the apartheid claim from the 1980s reemerged to support the war crimes claim that was added in support of what became the Goldstone Commission. From day one, that campaign has been targeting U.S. companies to get them to boycott Israel, adding various claims against Israel along the way thus making response a moving target, yet the overall objective remains the same. Boycott efforts targeting major companies such as Motorola and Caterpillar have failed in a large part due to my efforts showing that joining the Arab boycott of Israel is illegal.

The boycott campaign against major companies had two fronts. First, its supporters demanded those companies stop doing business either with or within Israel. Many companies conduct research and development in Israel, which among other things is a high tech center; therefore, these companies leaving Israel would not be in anyone's best interests. Second, they demanded businesses not to sell to Israel, which would also be silly from a business standpoint since Israel is a major consumer of American goods.

These companies are not chosen by accident; rather, they were specifically picked in order to destroy Israel's infrastructure. From a broad perspective, the loss of high tech development in Israel would be devastating to Israel's economy, and the Arabs know this. On the individual business level, removing certain technologies from Israel would harm its growth and economic prosperity. Boycott acquiescence by Motorola could harm the communications vital to Israel's existence since Israel uses their products. At the same time, boycott acquiescence by Caterpillar would harm Israel's infrastructure as growth and maintenance would be stunted.

These companies, among others, know Israel is a good customer and strategic partner in their growth. They also know joining the Arab boycott is illegal and even if it weren't, the boycott is just not in their best interests. This is why those direct boycott campaigns were rejected.

In response, the newest plan is to get Palestinians and their supporters to quietly purchase stock in businesses that they target in their boycott attempts and then donate the stock to their cause. The plan is to acquire enough voting stock to steal control of the boards of those companies.

To accomplish that, one of the 'end the occupation' groups has established an arrangement with an online stock trading site, and they are asking their supporters to buy securities in Caterpillar, primarily. After the purchase, they want people to deposit the stock in their trading account. They want free stock so they can have a vote on the boards of these companies. These people have no real vested interest in the success of those companies; rather, they want those companies to fail because they are important to Israel, which may suggest some impropriety on their part should they succeed. In fact, these people want to use their voting power to destroy the businesses if they do not boycott Israel.

This strategy is an active attempt to internally sabotage these companies at the expense of other shareholders simply because the companies that sell to Israel, Israeli companies or have offices in Israel. The campaign will once again fail because its supporters will not get enough votes to have any real affect, but they will become a major annoyance. As a result, there may be some nominal shareholder fears, which in turn may result in a small drop in stock price, but this will be nothing significant. Even if they do not gain control of those companies, they want to have as many people as possible who can speak at shareholder meetings and push the company to divest from Israel, or at the very least use it as a platform to lie and embarrass corporate officers. They will use the proverbial 'why do you still beat your wife?' questions to make a mockery of those shareholder meetings and try to prevent any real questions from investment shareholders. Questions during shareholder meetings and conference calls are usually reserved for larger institutional traders and the media. In many cases, smaller shareholders must submit their questions in writing. Moderators will generally ignore politically motivated questions such as those by the divestment shareholders. Based on their track record, I expect to see the divestment crowd disturbing the shareholder meetings with protests to get media attention, thereby drawing attention to their cause, which is the primary reason they are buying shares in the first place. They are not buying stock to invest.

The plan to destroy these companies internally will fail because the Board of Directors of every company has the fiduciary responsibility to ensure the best interests of the shareholders. No corporate board member will engage in internal sabotage of a company since it will result in headaches from the Securities and Exchange Commission. Such conduct is against the law.

The Methodology

I do not have a crystal ball. I do not need one. The Palestinians have already telegraphed their campaign methodology—the Boyle plan. First, there is the divest-from-Israel campaign which is divided into three phases:

1. Create divestment campaigns on campuses nationally that are bolstered with apartheid, war crimes, and other false claims.

2. Just as the campus campaign in the 1980s created an adult population which now accepts the idea of a Palestinian state, they want to create a generation that will boycott Israel and Jewish businesses with the ultimate goal of forcing Israel into financial ruin.

3. As Boyle stated, he wants to "dismantle" Israel, which the
    Arabs want to accomplish with the denial of financial bailouts
    after they crush Israel's economy. The Arab world wants to
    tell the world Israel was a mistake, it is a drain to the entire
    world, and therefore the world will be better off if this small
    country is removed from the map. They want the world pow-
    ers to do their dirty work for them, if at all possible.

The Arabs will simply not accept the fact that Israel exists and is here
to stay.

Boycotting Jewish Businesses Outside Israel

The Arab boycott continues to target American businesses owned or led by
Jews, regardless of the business having or not having any connection to Israel.
There are several websites promoting such boycotts, and the ones publishing
lists of companies to boycott are overwhelmingly based outside of the U.S. to
avoid violating U.S. Antiboycott laws; still, these websites are clearly aimed
towards the American audience. This is further proof the Arab boycott coor-
dinators are aware of the laws and are actively working around it. The same
websites advocate the academic boycott of Israel, and you can expect to see
more of that.

Palestinians and their supporters criticize many websites for being even
slightly pro-Israel since, on occasion, there may be a single pro-Israel comment on the site. On the Boycott Watch website, for example, there have been
articles criticizing Israeli websites and defending the Islamic Eid holiday post-
age stamp, yet some pro-Palestinian websites have criticized Boycott Watch
for being a "Zionist website." It is not that I mind the Boycott Watch being
called Zionist, but Boycott Watch is a consumer website. The fact that some
have vilified it for having even one pro-Israel article illustrates the witch hunt
for Zionists within the Arab world. To them, anything Zionist is evil regardless of the overall content, and they attack websites which have any pro-Israel
content, regardless of the focus. It is not just websites. Palestinians regularly

complain to media outlets for reporting any pro-Israel opinions, even when the same media outlet has a clear bias in favor of the Palestinians.

New Occupation Claims

Despite Israel's evacuation from Gaza, articles continue to be published claiming to be written in the "occupied Gaza strip." The authors continue to blame Israel for everything that could possibly go wrong, despite there being no Jewish presence there. Using the occupation claim in the by-line of an article may endear certain readers, but it also establishes the bias of the writer and publication. Of course, the tactic is meant to establish *de facto* blame on Israel without any proof of the claim. Despite there being no occupation, since Israel is neither in Gaza nor in the areas the Palestinians have agreed is there own, plus the fact that the Palestinian Authority is bound by agreements as to which land belongs to them, Palestinian supporters continue to make the nonsensical claim that proves they want all of Israel.

Israel Apartheid Week

Israel Apartheid Week occurs on campuses at various times throughout the year, depending on when a campus group wants to promote it. Usually the event occurs in the spring as close to Israel's Independence Day as possible, in order to disrupt the festivities of Jewish groups. Nothing is new in these campaigns. You can count on seeing Israeli apartheid claims, hearing stories about how Israelis torture Palestinians, and listening to garbage of how land was stolen from Palestinians. They naturally won't tell you the apartheid claims are false; nor will they tell you Jews purchased the land which title records support; nor will they tell you that Israeli civil law covers all people including Palestinians. They do not want you to know Israel is a democracy where every claim can be made to a court of law. They will, however, make claims they cannot backup and will make impassioned claims to get sympathy.

Simply making a claim does not make it automatically valid. Israel Apartheid Week is primarily a recruitment tool. They use the unfounded charges to get people to hate Israel. Most Jewish students feel intimidated by those events and stay clear, which is what the Palestinians want; however, I have a response. I suggest students sponsor Middle East Human Rights Weeks, where they talk about how Muslim women cannot vote or drive, how Jews are forbidden from entering Arab counties, how it is unsafe for Jews who are allowed in, how Christian tourists are forbidden from entering most of Saudi Arabia and especially Mecca and Medina, how Jews and Christians in Arab lands are subject to Islamic Dhimmi laws which force Jews to only walk on the 'impure' side of Muslims, and how both Christians and Jews living in Islamic nations must pay a special tax for not being Muslim. The fact is, the only Middle East nation which allows people of every religion to vote is Israel; people need to know where the real discrimination can be found. Moral people should not allow the immoral lies against Israel to go unchecked. The real discrimination exists in the Arab nations and it is against Christians too, not just Jews.

The Nakba

To the Palestinians, Israeli Independence Day was "the disaster," or Nakba in Arabic; to them, it was a disaster because a Jewish state was established. This name alone speaks volumes. It shows how the Palestinians refuse to accept the mere existence of Israel. They do not want a Palestinian-Arab state alongside Israel; rather, they want it in place of Israel. Their Nakba is Israel's very existence and the celebration of it signals how the Palestinians will perpetually vilify and attack Israel as long as it exists.

These campaigns, however, never stand alone. As with the Israel Apartheid Week, they mix and match events and anti-Israel claims as often as they can, thereby throwing off the pro-Israel side.

False Quote Syndrome

Palestinians and their supporters are now distributing articles and quotes by prominent Jews, most notably Albert Einstein, that give the impressions the authors were against the establishment of Israel in 1948. There is only one problem with these quotes—many of them are complete fabrications. Albert Einstein was instrumental in the establishment of Israel; so much so, that he was asked to be the first President of the State of Israel, an offer he declined. Albert Einstein worked with Dr. Chaim Weizmann to establish the Hebrew University of Jerusalem, and he left his documents and papers to the school in his will.

The Albert Einstein College of Medicine is the prominent medical school of Yeshiva University. Yeshiva University has always been a Zionistic school, and Mr. Einstein agreed to allow his name to be used for the medical school in 1953. Had Mr. Einstein not been Zionistic, neither party would have wanted to be associated with each other by name. So when you hear the claims about Mr. Einstein, you know they are a complete fabrication.

This is but one example of purposely created false quotes. The most important thing to remember is that even if such a quote is true, it is irrelevant. Besides, Jews, just as with any group, have the right to disagree, and we often do. The goal of the Palestinians is to present you with a false quote and then ask you what you think of it, thereby trying to trip you up with something of which you probably never thought. The main purpose of their technique is to insinuate the ideas of one person inherently invalidate Israel's legitimacy. That is absurd.

Having a handful of people who disagree is not actually a negative. The United States, for example, is nearly split in half politically. Palestinians and their supporters have found so few Jews who are anti-Israel, statistically near zero, that they have had to falsify quotes to claim any mainstream Jewish support. Even if the quotes are true, they are statistically irrelevant. My response, therefore, is to ask the Palestinians if this is their best argument. If so, I ask them if people in Iran, Syria, Libya, Saudi Arabia and other Arab countries are even allowed to express opinions contrary dictators who run those countries. Since dissent with the government is not allowed in those countries, that ends the conversation. If they try to lie and claim freedom of speech in Arab countries, I laugh.

Neturei Karta: Man Bites Dog

You may have seen them in the media, a group of Hassidic orthodox Jews with long coats and beards protesting against Israel and carrying Palestinian flags. That is the Neturei Karta, meaning Guardians of the City, referring to Jerusalem, a small group that is oddly named because they do anything but guard Jerusalem. They primarily live in one small Jerusalem suburb, yet they do not believe in Israel as a state.

In the United States, they claim to number in the hundreds or thousands, but they really number about twenty. They always get media attention when they protest against Israel because they are a complete oddity. They claim to be following Jewish law, yet violate it every step of the way, including being opposed to the biblical phrase that all Jews use in prayer: "From Zion shall go forth Torah, and the word of G-d from Jerusalem" (Isaiah 2:3). They say they are Jews against Zionism, yet the two cannot be separated.

When I attended the Israel hate-fest at Georgetown University, Neturei Karta members were there, but nobody was talking to them for the same reason they love media photo opportunities, but rarely comment—these people are neither well spoken nor have anything worthwhile to say. All they really want is to be seen in the media. At Georgetown during the Jewish Sabbath, those who attended were clearly violating several basic Jewish laws, including carrying outside on the Sabbath, and not attending prayer services. They left mid-day Saturday, returning Sunday morning for their threatened mass protest that was actually attended by fewer than ten people, which is common for their protests. Their oddity attracts media attention which gives the false impression they are a much larger group.

They made the news when they flew to Iran in 2006 to lend moral support and praise for Iranian President Mahmoud Ahmadinejad and his plans to destroy Israel. After returning, they faced heavy criticism in their own greater Jewish community in Monsey, New York, especially from other Hassidic Jews. Reports say that many businesses refused to allow them and their families in stores, and as a result some wives left their husbands, with their kids, because of the pressure. Six months later, there was an electrical fire in their Monsey, New York synagogue, destroying it. The general Jewish population despises this hate group so much that other Hassidic Jews danced on the synagogues front lawn while the firefighters were putting the fire out. A week later, I tried to see the building, but police were keeping cars and pedestrian traffic away from the building because the traffic jams from onlookers had become too much of a traffic safety problem.

Neturei Karta members are despised by other Jews, and they have no actual rabbinical guidance. There is not one leading rabbi anywhere in the world that approves their actions or guides them. To Jews, they are as absurd as seeing a protest to ban air or water. They are absurd, and the fact that the Neturei Karta has such a minute membership speaks volumes. Judaism accepts different points of view, as indicated by the number of branches within Judaism and the diverse political views amongst Jews; still, the Neturei Karta is largely despised and ignored as a fringe and quite frankly stupid group. Of course Palestinians love the Neturei Karta, since they appear to present a Jewish religious justification for their radical beliefs; however, knowing the Neturei Karta membership is miniscule actually makes the Palestinians and their supporters look brainless for accepting their help. The Neturei Karta gets media attention strictly because they are such an oddity. A dog biting a man is not news. A man biting a dog is news because it is ironic and strange. So, too, is the Neturei Karta.

Iranian President Mahmoud Ahmadinejad

Iran is unquestionably a player in the Middle-East peace process, or in this case, peace prevention. Ahmadinejad's threats to destroy Israel is real, and he picked up where Saddam Hussein left off, with one real difference—Iran is on a verifiable path to building weapons of mass destruction. Just like Egyptian President Gamal Abdel Nasser, Libya's Colonel Muammar Al-Gaddafi, Syria's Hafez al-Assad, and Iraqi President Saddam Hussein before him, Iranian President Mahmoud Ahmadinejad wants to be the single ruler of a unified Arab world and he is rallying the masses around his vision to destroy Israel.

The power struggles within the Arab world have existed long before the creation of the modern Arab states, borders for which were drawn by nations that had no care for where any tribes lived. The world sees this problem in Iraq with the ethnic Kurds, for example, who one day found themselves as an oppressed minority within their own land. The internal and external power struggles prevent unification in the Arab world as is evident by the struggle for democracy within Iraq. This is especially true in Lebanon, which has a power-sharing constitution that is always under assault by Muslims who have assassinated their Christian counterparts.

Ahmadinejad has not yet built enough personal clout in the Arab world to be the singular leader, and he is betting that destroying Israel will help him achieve such a position. Like the suicide bombers before him, he wants to martyr himself and does not care if that means by a retaliatory Israeli nuclear strike. As long as Jews die, then it does not matter what happens to his countrymen. That is what makes him so dangerous, which some people fail to see. In the Cold War, the United States and Soviet Union refrained from using nuclear weapons because the Mutual Assured Destruction doctrine meant one missile launch would result in countless launches from the other side in response long before any missile left a nation's internal border. Since Ahmadinejad does not care about his own destruction or the destruction of his own nation and people, he would not hesitate to launch nuclear weapons against Israel if given the opportunity.

Palestinians are unfortunately not concerned with what the West sees as an Ahmadinejad threat, because they see their own demise as martyrdom so long as Israel is wiped off the map in the process. That coupled with the fact that Ahmadinejad is Persian and not Arab makes the possibility of him ruling the Arab world only possible if he uses nuclear or other weapons of mass destruction against Israel. I believe the reason Palestinians in America do not protest against Ahmadinejad, is the same reason they do not protest him in the Middle East—they view Ahmadinejad as a viable path to Israel's destruction, to which they do not object.

Israel may soon have no choice but to attack Iran. While that may result in conventional warfare with neighboring countries, the resulting ground war would far better than Israel being hit with nuclear weapons. Meanwhile, the vilification of Israel persists, especially within the Israel divestment and boycott groups. These people are more interested in where Jews want to build houses in Jerusalem, than preventing nuclear war, as they are distracting people from the global threat of nuclear fallout, all in the false name of peace.

Disturb And Disrupt Venues

The old adage of actions speaking louder than words is muted when disrespect becomes the norm. It is not uncommon to have hecklers in audiences when pro-Israel speakers come to campuses. Conversely, there have been a few cases where a pro-Israel supporter makes a comment and is immediately ejected from Palestinian events, as was the case with Bill Maniaci at the Georgetown University Hate-Fest.

Pro-Palestinian groups love to silence, heckle and even abuse pro-Israel speakers to the point where it is almost expected. In February, 2009 Israeli Ambassador Michael Oren was repeatedly heckled when he spoke at U.C. Irvine, all in the name of Palestinians claiming to want peace. Naturally, disrespect is the antithesis of attaining peace, but that did not curtail the outbursts which some people in the audience, apparently including the U.C. Irvine Police Department, feared would turn to violence. Many arrests were made and a professor at the university had to demand decorum for twenty minutes as Ambassador Oren waited off-stage.

The tactic of silencing pro-Israel speakers not only indicates a lack of legitimate response and counterclaims, but is also reminiscent of fascism, which silences all opposition. Once again, such actions stand in opposition to achieving peace.

Sabeel—The Religious Equivalent of Cross-dressing

I first came across the Sabeel organization when I was undercover at the Divest from Israel conference at Georgetown University, or as I like to call it, the Georgetown Israel Hate-Fest. On the last day, an organizer of Sabeel was passing out information about an upcoming event he was hosting. I forget his name, but I asked him what Sabeel is, and he told me it is the "ecumenical divestment campaign." This caught my attention since I had sat through a session where Muslims were telling Christians to lie to their clergy to bring the divestment campaign into churches.

Sabeel publicly claims to advocate a two-state solution, but it is staunchly pro-divestment, thus it wants to destroy Israel economically. Sabeel has an interesting angle for its campaign.

Despite claiming to be a Christian group, Sabeel's name translates to "the way" from Arabic. Sabeel is rooted in the Islamic philosophy of the Jewish Bible/Christian Old Testament as being an illegitimate and bastardized version of the Koran, despite the fact that the Bible pre-dates Islam. As such, Islam believes Judaism, and therefore Christianity, are invalid. Sabeel is an attempt to extend the Islamic teaching that Judaism and its tie to the land of Israel are fabrications, as is evident in Sabeel's teachings of "Liberation Theology." While some Christian sects teach Replacement Theology, meaning the New

Testament replaced Jews as the chosen people of the Bible, Sabeel teaches a version of Liberation Theology, in which it wants to see the Bible liberated from the Jews, thus eliminating what they see as the pesky claim of Jews to the land of Israel.

According to its own website where one can read about how the organization was formed at www.sabeel.org, they "convened a committee... to explore ways in which this theology could be developed..." In this statement, it admits to having created the theology by exploring ways to push its agenda via religion; in other words, Sabeel invented a religion philosophy to advance its politics. Perhaps this explains why, as addressed in Chapter Twelve, Muslim students had no problem telling Christians to lie to their clergy, to which Sabeel not only did not object, but surely was an active part of the "Christian Outreach" seminar. Sabeel and its Liberation Theology are nothing more than another falsified campaign to destroy Israel.

To their credit, Christians welcome in virtually everyone who wants to be part of their religion. In the eyes of Palestinians, this open attitude also opens the door to the perversion of religion by people who use politics to abuse the church, but Christians are smarter than Palestinians give them credit. While some Christians may front Sabeel, it is really about the Islamic push to destroy Israel. This group especially wants peace-activist college students who generally wear jeans and t-shirts to dress up and play the part of conservative Christians to bring the political campaign into churches under false pretenses.

Food Co-ops

The Arab plan is to poison impressionable minds, planting the seeds of stealth-hate amongst as many people as possible. Of course, they do not tell people they are really trying to destroy Israel, but instead claim they are bringing peace to the Middle East. They are purposely deceiving people and getting them to do their dirty work for them. There is a reason, therefore, why food co-ops are popular and even planned targets for the Israel boycotters. Peace and social activists tend to gravitate to co-ops because they are, by definition, cooperatives; thus, people are supposed to work together and have business input without any of the financial responsibility that comes with it. Since there is no single owner of a co-op, there is no person or family who has staked their time and money to build the co-op business.

This makes the co-op a prime recruitment target for Israel boycotters. Members vote about products sold and store policies, not individual business-people who are concerned with their own personal livelihood; therefore, the people who vote may have zero personal business stake in the co-op. In some cases, they join for cost savings, which do not really exist anyhow since members work at the co-op for the discounts. In many cases, co-op members would be better off taking a part-time job because then they would have more product choices for the equal pay they would have received had they worked at a real job rather than performing required "volunteering" at the co-op, but I digress.

I have been involved with the blocking of Israel boycott attempts co-ops across the country, sometimes directly and sometimes consulting with the Antiboycotters. In each case, the boycott attempt has been blocked by citing the U.S. Antiboycott law. The best way to combat the boycott, be it at co-ops or not, is to ask for Israeli products at the stores you shop. While there is nothing wrong with stores that may not carry any Israeli products, if you are told the store specifically boycotts Israeli products, then there is a problem.

Conclusion

Palestinians hide the truth behind their Israel boycott campaign by recruiting potential Israel boycott advocates and masking their campaign in a cloak of false peace possibilities. After I exposed the divest-from-Israel campaign as being an illegal foreign boycott, that campaign was renamed to "Boycott Divestment Sanctions" to make people think that divestment is not boycott, which it still is by definition since divesting is the removal of business dealings. The BDS campaign, as they like to call it, added sanctions as a distraction. It is another bait and switch, the same way the Palestinians add the word evil when referring to the false apartheid claim. You may recall from Chapter Five, where I exposed the technique of distracting the audience into agreeing apartheid is evil, while simultaneously blaming Israel for utilizing such conduct. In an argument, Arabs and their supporters will discredit their opponents by asking questions like, "How can you say apartheid is not evil," as if everyone universally accepts Israel as being apartheid. The same bait and switch tactic is used to insert the word "sanctions" into the argument while claiming divestment is not a boycott. When you discuss the Israel boycott as being illegal, they will take two out of three and argue divestment and sanctions, distracting you from the main argument. However, their claim for sanctions is based on the illegal boycott and divestment call.

There will be more boycott campaigns targeting different companies. That is the part of plan Boyle created and advocates as a method of destroying Israel's economy, as well as to debase Israel's right to exist and remove Israel as a legitimate state in the eyes of the United Nations. It all goes back to Arab plan to destroy Israel by using the plan that Boyle created as part of his legal practice with the PLO as his client.

As you may recall from Chapter Six, Boyle's plan includes steps to "immediately move for the *de facto* suspension of Israel throughout the entirety of the United Nations system, including the General Assembly and all U.N. subsidiary organs and bodies." In doing this, Boyle is stating he wants to delegitimize Israel as a nation. If this were to come to pass, Arab attacks on Israel would not be considered acts of war. This suspension would inherently allow any government in the world to claim the land of Israel as theirs. Israel would thus cease to exist on the international stage, if Boyle gets his way.

Boyle, in his own words, stated he created the "Divestment Campaign Against Israel." The BDS campaign is completely based on the Boyle plan. Since he created and promoted his plan as part of his official work for the Palestine Liberation Organization, it is part of the official Arab boycott of Israel and therefore constitutes an illegal foreign boycott. While the boycott advocates will always claim they are pro-peace, the fact is they are not. Many of the BDS advocates have been tricked into accepting the claim that separating people will somehow bring them together, but that is impossible. You simply cannot divide people to bring them together. History has proven economic cooperation is the key to sustaining peace, which is why the Arab boycott must end before there can ever be peace in the Middle East, or anywhere else in the world for that matter. You simply cannot have peace with people you will not sit down with for a cup of coffee.

In order to achieve peace, there must be something to sustain that peace— a reason people will not consider war. A good reason is mutual economic reliance. Lasting peace can only happen when the price of war exceeds the value of lost peace. If you cannot afford war, peace is the only option. The Arab boycott of Israel, therefore, must end immediately.

Epilog

After this book was completed and before it has gone to press, the Arab dismantlement plan for Israel has become known as de-legitimization. Arabs want to have average Americans to do their bidding to bankrupt Israel so they can then say Israel is a failed state which needs to be dismantled rather than bailed out. Meanwhile, haters of Israel continue to hide their true goals as if the PA/PLO map of their "Palestine" was not the map of all of Israel, yet as we see in the official PA/PLO logo, their goal is to replace all of Israel.

The fact is, the only way to fulfill the hate-filled dream of a Palestinian state replacing Israel is to murder every Israeli. Perhaps this explains why the Arab world refused to recognize Israel, as doing so will be a de facto recognition that their dream is impossible. I have some news for those who wish to destroy Israel and the Jews. It's been tried before and we prevailed every time while the attackers have become mere footnotes in history. Israel is here to stay.

Appendix A—The Arab Plan to Destroy Israel

This diagram illustrates the history of how the Arab boycott of Israel and divestment campaign are related.

Notice how Boyle changed the direction of the boycott and the action loop he created until the Goldstone report. This is their plan and methodology. They can run two major campaigns simultaneously and will circle everything back to the Arab boycott with plans to destroy Israel at every turn. Notice how there are no actual peace initiatives in their plan.

Bibliography

Jerusalem 1913: The Origins of the Arab-Israeli Conflict by Amy Dockser Marcus

The Jewish Virtual Library—A service of the American-Israeli Cooperative Enterprise: http://www.jewishvirtuallibrary.org

CIA World Factbook: www.cia.gov

The Politically Incorrect Guide to Islam (and the Crusades) by Robert Spencer

The Palestine Yearbook (1945), published by the Zionist Organization of America

Americans for Middle East Understanding (http://www.ameu.org) article: "Law and Disorder in the Middle East" by Francis Anthony Boyle, January 2002

Counterpunch magazine (www.counterpunch.org) article: "In Defense of a Divestment Campaign Against Israel" by Francis Anthony Boyle, May of 2002

Peace Under Fire—Various articles, Verso Books

"The Socialism of Fools: The Left, the Jews and Israel" by Dr. Seymour Martin Lipset, *Encounter* magazine, December, 1969 (page 24)

About the Author

Photo by Pollack Studio, South Euclid, Ohio.

After years as a political activist, top technical consultant and businessman, Fred Taub created Boycott Watch in 2002 to combat false information in consumer boycotts spread over the Internet and soon discovered the Arab boycott of Israel was the single biggest boycott in the world, yet forgotten about in the U.S. while the Arab world quietly enforcing it with the express purpose of destroying Israel via economic warfare.

Fred Taub is a life-long activist who is first concerned with getting to the truth. He ran a successful campaign to deport Nazi John "Ivan the Terrible" Demjanjuk and testified in a First Amendment court case in support of simultaneous protest and against the head of the Ohio Ku Klux Klan. That case was won before the Ohio Supreme Court. Even before creating Boycott Watch, his articles have been published globally, and he was soon after recognized as an expert in boycotts. He has broken several news stories, including in the Natalee Holloway case. He has appeared as an expert guest on the Fox News Channel and Al-Jazeera Television, been a guest on numerous major radio stations, been quoted in the Wall Street Journal, L.A. Times, and USA Today to name just a few. Most impressively, Boycott Watch has been cited in two cases before the United States Supreme Court as the authority in boycotts.

While Fred Taub originated the arguments against the divest-from-Israel campaign, Boycotting Peace serves as the ultimate guide to combating the scourge of hatred against Jews, falsely masked as a peace campaign. He exposes both people and methodologies, including the direct link between the Palestinian campaign to lie to churches, the direct involvement of Yasir Arafat in the Arab boycott of Israel campaign while claiming to negotiate for peace in good faith, the rejection of proposed Palestinian state and the U.N. Gaza/Goldstone commission. It is an eye-opening must read for anyone who truly wants to see peace in the Middle East.